STRENGTH TRAINING FOR WOMEN

BUILDING POWER AND GRACE

BY

MUJAHID BAKHT

Hardcover: ISBN: 978-1-961299-75-7
Paperback: ISBN: 978-1-961299-76-4
EBook: ISBN: 978-1-961299-77-1
Audiobook   ISBN: 978-1-961299-78-8

Published by
Atlas Amazon, LLC

United States of America

Copyright © 2023 by Mujahid Bakht

All rights reserved. No part of this book, "Strength Training for women: Building power and grace", may be reproduced, stored in a retrieval system, or transmitted in any form or by any means, electronic, mechanical, photocopying, recording, or otherwise, without the prior written permission of the publisher, except in the case of brief quotations embodied in critical articles or reviews. For permission requests, write to the publisher, addressed "Attention: Permissions Coordinator," at the following address:

Atlas Amazon, LLC.

244 Fifth Avenue, Suite D210

New York, NY 10001 USA

The main goal of Mujahid Bakht's book "Strength Training for Women" is to close the knowledge gap between contemporary, evidence-based strength training methods and outdated beliefs about women's fitness. Mujahid Bakht wants to dispel the myths and false beliefs that have prevented women for a long time from discovering the many advantages of weightlifting, including increased bone density and better muscular tone.

With an emphasis on women's bodies, the book fills in as an exhaustive aid for exploring the universe of strength training. It features the meaning of legitimate procedure, the role job sustenance plays, and the effect a very well-planned training routine has on women' general well-being and health. By bestowing how he might interpret female physiology, Mujahid intends to furnish women with the capacities and information expected for secure, successful, and sure training.

Furthermore, Mujahid Bakht aspires to inspire a new generation of strong, empowered women who embrace strength training not just as a form of exercise but also as a testament to their potential, resilience, and grace via the stories of real women and their transformational journeys.

TABLE OF CONTENTS

CHAPTER 1 15
INTRODUCTION TO STRENGTH TRAINING 15
The benefits of strength training for women 17
Debunking myths about weightlifting and femininity 20

CHAPTER 2 25
THE FEMALE PHYSIOLOGY AND STRENGTH TRAINING 25
Hormonal differences and their impact on training 25
Muscle fiber type distribution and growth potential 29
The menstrual cycle and training considerations 30

CHAPTER 3 34
SETTING CLEAR GOALS 34
Defining your purpose aesthetic, health, performance 34
The importance of realistic goal setting 38

CHAPTER 4 42
ESSENTIAL EQUIPMENT AND GYM FAMILIARITY 42
Home gym vs. commercial gym: Pros and Cons 42
Must-have equipment for effective training 46

CHAPTER 5 52
CORE STRENGTH TRAINING PRINCIPLES 52

Progressive overload explained 52

Importance of rest and recovery 55

Balancing volume and intensity 59

CHAPTER 6 63

FORM AND TECHNIQUE MASTERY 63

Why correct form matters 63

Tips for common exercises like squats, deadlifts, and presses 66

CHAPTER 7 71

BUILDING A SOLID FOUNDATION – THE BEGINNER'S PLAN 71

Compound movements 71

A sample 8-week beginner's strength training program 75

CHAPTER 8 80

NUTRITIONAL STRATEGIES FOR MUSCLE GROWTH AND FAT LOSS 80

Importance of hydration 83

Supplements: Which are beneficial? 87

CHAPTER 9 94

ADVANCED TECHNIQUES AND PLATEAU BREAKING 94

Incorporating techniques like drop sets, supersets, and paused reps 95

How to recognize and overcome training plateaus 100

CHAPTER 10 104

STRENGTH TRAINING DURING PREGNANCY AND POSTPARTUM 104

Safe exercise recommendations during each trimester 104

Regaining strength and muscle post-pregnancy 106

CHAPTER 11 111

STRENGTH TRAINING FOR MATURE WOMEN 111

Addressing hormonal changes during menopause 112

Bone health and osteoporosis prevention.............................116

Adjustments and considerations for older adults.................120

CHAPTER 12 128

INJURY PREVENTION AND MANAGEMENT..............128

Common injuries in strength training..................................128

Warm-ups, cool-downs, and flexibility's role in injury prevention 135

How to train around injuries 139

CHAPTER 13 145

INCORPORATING CARDIO AND FLEXIBILITY.........145

The role of cardiovascular training in a strength-focused routine 146

Static vs. dynamic stretching: When and how to use them .. 150

CHAPTER 14 156

TRACKING PROGRESS AND ADJUSTING YOUR PLAN 156

The importance of logging workouts 156

How to measure progress 163

Adjusting your training based on feedback and results 169

CHAPTER 15 175

CELEBRATING STRENGTH - STORIES FROM REAL WOMEN 175

Inspirational stories of women who transformed their lives through strength training 176

How strength training empowers women in various aspects of life 180

CONCLUSION 186

ABOUT AUTHOR

Mr. Mujahid Bakht, Profile:-

LIFE HISTORY:- Mr. Bakht is a mature, experienced, extremely enthusiastic, energetic, administrator and thirty-six years have proven experience as a businessman in international marketing and public relations. Mr. Bakht is an International Real Estate Specialist, and Professional Business and Projects Consultant. He was born in Pakistan, Educated in Pakistan and USA. Presently American Citizen belongs to the business-oriented family. Thirty-Seven years Resident of New York, USA.

BUSINESS HISTORY:- Mr. Bakht is a Founder & President of Atlas Amazon, LLC., Mr. Bakht is a business developer and multilingual business specialist in the Caribbean, South East Asia, and the Middle East emerging markets Mr. Bakht has served, met, and host many "Heads of the Countries" Also, maintain a close relationship with investors of high net worth in the USA.

CAREER:- Mr. Bakht has been engaged with many multinational companies in the field of international real estate investment, communication, technology, diamond, gold, mining, Pre-Feb housing, wind & solar energy, outsourcing management, and project consulting along with business partners & associates worldwide. Mr. Bakht has participated in major national and international conferences including participated in United Nations (U.N.O.) conferences.

TRAVEL:- Mr. Bakht is well-traveled and has visited many countries worldwide.

MANAGEMENT EXPERIENCE:- Thirty-Seven years of diversified experience in project consulting, marketing, and business management. As a Director of Marketing, Director of Public Relations, Director of International Affairs, Executive Vice President, President, CEO, and Chairman of many national & multinational companies, where he served previously. Mr. Bakht hired and trained many professionals as business consultants in international marketing and supervised them. Mr. Bakht is the author and publisher of multiple books.

CERTIFICATES; Certificate of Authenticity from Bill Rodham Clinton, President of the United States, and Hillary Rodham Clinton First Lady, USA. (July 20, 2000);

CERTIFICATE OF ACHIEVEMENT; Achievement Award was presented to Mr. Bakht by Stephen Fossler for five years of continued growth and customer satisfaction from 1996 to 2001.

HONORS MEMBER; Madison Who's Who of Professionals, having demonstrated exemplary achievement and distinguished contributions to the business community, registered at the Library of Congress in Washington D.C. USA. (2007 & 2008)

HONORS MEMBER; Premiere Who's Who International, professional business executive having demonstrated exemplary achievement and distinguished contributions to the International business community, 2008 and 2009.

CERTIFICATE OF AUTHENTICITY; from Terence R. McAuliffe, Chairman of Democratic National Committee, Tom Dachle, Senate Democratic Leader, Dick Gephardt, House Democratic Leader, USA. (June 16, 2001);

CERTIFICATE OF AUTHENTICITY; from Terence R.

McAuliffe, Chairman of Democratic National Committee, USA. (April 16, 2002).

PERSONAL HISTORY:- Mr. Bakht married in the year of 1992 in New York City, USA. He is a Father of three children, all three were Born raised, and educated in the United States of America.

Dartmouth College, New Hampshire, USA.
St. John University, Queens, New York, USA.
Syracuse University, Upstate New York, USA.

MEETINGS WITH DIGNITARIES AND HEADS OF THE COUNTRIES

Honorable. Teng-Hui-Lee, President of Taiwan. 1999.
Hon. Leonard Fernandez, President of the Dominican Republic. 1999.
Prince. Ahmed Fahad Al-Turki, (Saudi Arabia). 2000.
Benazir Bhutto, Prime Minister of Pakistan, 2001.
Dr. Keith Mitchell, Prime Minister of Grenada, West Indies. 2003-2004.
Pierre Charles, Prime Minister of Dominica, West Indies, 2003.
Mr. Charles Sovran, Foreign Minister of Dominica, 2003.

Robert H. O. Corbin Leader & Deputy-Prime-Minister (PNC) Guyana 2004.

Hon. P. J. Peterson, Prime Minister of Jamaica. 2004.

Dr. Kenny D. Anthony, Prime Minister of Saint Lucia, West Indies. 2005.

Hon. Owen Arthur, Prime Minister of Barbados, West Indies. 2005.

Michael de la Bastide, "Chief Justice" and President of the Caribbean Islands. 2005.

Mahmood M. Hussain, the Private Office of His Royal Highness. Dr. Sheikh-

Sultan Bin Khalifa Bin Zayed Al Nahyan, Abu-Dhabi, U.A.E. 2005.

Sultan S. Al Mansoori, Saeed & Mohammed Alnaboodah, Dubai, UAE 2005.

Ibrahim A. Gambari, Under-Secretary-General (United Nations) 2006.

Hon. Villasarao Deshmukh, Chief Minister of Maharashtra, India, 2006.

Hon. Ashok Chovan, Minister of Industries, Maharashtra, India, 2006.

Hon. Liu Bowie, Ambassador of China, United Nations, 2006.

Senator Einstein Louison, Ministry of Agriculture,

Grenada.

Hon. Mark Isaac, Minister of State, Grenada, West Indies.

Hon. Brenda Hood, Minister for Tourism, Civil Aviation, Culture, Grenada.

Wayne Smith, Mayor, Township of Irvington, New Jersey, USA.

Orlando J. Moreno, Brigadier General & Military Advisor, (UNO) Venezuela.

CHAPTER 1

INTRODUCTION TO STRENGTH TRAINING

You know that feeling when you open a heavy door, and for a brief moment, you pause, surprised by your strength? Or when you hoist up a packed suitcase and think, "Wow, I did that!" It's exhilarating, right? Power isn't just about bulging biceps or toned abs; it's about those everyday moments when our bodies surprise us. And that's where strength training comes into play.

Strength training, often imagined with burly men lifting astronomical weights in dimly lit gyms, is as much a woman's game as it is a man's. Women, just like men, have been endowed with muscles. Why not understand and use them to their full potential?

If you've been on the fence about whether or not to delve into strength training, here are some compelling reasons to start:

1. Busting the 'Bulky' Myth: Let's get one thing straight - lifting weights will not make you hulk out. Our bodies, women's bodies, just aren't designed that way. Instead, what strength training does is sculpt and define. Those toned arms or shapely legs you admire? They're crafted through consistent, balanced strength training.

2. Bone Health Matters: Remember when your mom told you to drink milk for strong bones? She was on the right track, but there's more to the story. Our bones may become less dense as we age, leading to conditions like osteoporosis. Lifting weights is a sure-shot way to keep those bones robust and sturdy.

3. Power up Your Metabolism: You know those days when you feel like you've gained weight just by looking at a cupcake? We've all been there. But here's a fun fact: muscle burns more calories at rest than fat. So, the more you build your muscles through strength training, the more you rev up your metabolic rate.

4. Strength for Daily Life: It's not just about looking good but also about feeling good in our daily tasks. From lugging groceries to rearranging furniture or playing with your kids, a substantial body makes life smoother.

5. Mind Over Muscle: Have you ever had a rough day and found solace in a workout? There's science behind that. Lifting weights, like any form of exercise, releases endorphins – our body's natural mood lifters. Beyond that, conquering a weight or achieving a personal best at the gym can do wonders for our confidence and mental resilience.

6. Stand Tall, Really: Remember being told to sit up straight? Strength training, especially exercises that target the core, goes a long way in improving posture. When you train regularly, you naturally stand a little taller, a little prouder.

7. Redefining Strength: Here's the heart of the matter. Strength training is transformative, not just physically, but mentally. As women, lifting weights can often feel like a rebellious act, a way to defy societal expectations. Every session, every weight lifted, is a reminder of what we're capable of.

In the coming chapters, we'll delve deeper into the intricacies of strength training. Whether you're a novice or someone looking to refine your knowledge, this guide aims to be your companion on this rewarding journey. Strength isn't just for the select few. It's a universal gift, and it's high time we, as women, claim it.

The benefits of strength training for women

The realm of strength training has often been dominated by visions of burly men lifting astronomical weights, but this perception is gradually changing. In recent years, more women are venturing into this space, realizing the transformative benefits that it offers. Let's discuss the myriad advantages of strength training for women:

1. Toned Physique, Not Bulkiness: One of the most common misconceptions about strength training for women is the fear of becoming 'too bulky.' In reality, due to hormonal differences, especially the lower levels of testosterone in women compared to men, women tend to develop lean and toned muscles rather than bulky ones.

2. Enhanced Bone Density: Women are at a higher risk of osteoporosis, especially post-menopause. Strength training puts stress on bones, stimulating osteoblasts, the cells responsible for bone formation. Regular weight-bearing exercises can significantly increase bone density, reducing the risk of fractures and breaks.

3. Boosted Metabolism: Muscle tissue is metabolically active, meaning it burns calories even at rest. By increasing lean muscle mass through strength training, women can boost their basal metabolic rate, which results in more effective calorie burning all day.

4. Utilitarian Strength: Lifting loads in an exercise center isn't the central part of strength training. Improving functional strength is fundamental for doing ordinary errands like moving furnishings, bringing up kids, and conveying food. A more muscular body ensures that these activities become simpler to perform and don't overwhelm the muscles.

5. Benefits for Emotional Wellness: Strength training and practice discharge endorphins, which are neuron chemicals that typically decrease torment and further develop a state of mind.

Following continuous strength instructional meetings, numerous women report feeling less anxious, more focused, and more sure.

6. Better Stance and Equilibrium: Activities zeroing in on reinforcing the center muscles are especially significant for further developing stance. Age and stationary ways of life usually lead to slumping, which can be avoided with a solid center and back. Strength training likewise upgrades balance, which brings down the possibility of falling.

7. Lower Hazard of Ongoing Sicknesses: Studies have associated obstruction with a reduced chance of a few constant circumstances, including type 2 diabetes, coronary illness, and hypertension. It contributes to better cholesterol levels, better glucose guidelines, and improved cardiovascular well-being.

8. Weight Control: Strength training can be a compelling technique for weight reduction and upkeep when matched with a nutritious eating routine and a high-impact workout. Acquiring muscle makes it simpler to keep up with or get in shape since power calorie consumption is higher than that of fat.

9. Upgraded Athletic Execution: Strength training can enormously expand power, speed, and perseverance in competitors and other genuinely dynamic individuals.

10. Strengthening: At long last, strength training has a huge mental advantage. It is enabling us to lift loads, set individual standards, and witness genuine development. Strength training transforms into a way for a ton of women to assume back command over their bodies, help confidence, and oppose society's standards.

In light of everything, strength training furnishes women with a great many benefits in the space of the body, brain, and soul. Strength training s significant, yet so is developing a more grounded, more satisfied, and versatile variant of oneself.

Debunking myths about weightlifting and femininity

When we discuss weightlifting, what strikes a chord? Prominent men have immense muscles, correct? Yet, what might be said about women? For quite a while, many individuals have accepted things about weightlifting and women that are false. We should discuss these fantasies and figure out reality.

Myth 1: Weightlifting Will make women Look Cumbersome

The Story: That's what specific individuals feel; assuming women lift loads, they will turn out to be exceptionally solid and seem to be male jocks.

The Truth: This isn't accurate. Women have, to a lesser extent, a chemical called testosterone than men. This chemical aids in building large muscles. Along these lines, women who lift loads get conditioned and solid but not massive. Rather than seeming to be muscle heads, they get a fit and sound look.

Myth 2: It Isn't Female to Weightlifting

The Story: Some say lifting loads is just for men rather than elegant.

The Truth: Who concludes what is refined? Each woman has the privilege to pick what she needs to do. It is delightful to Be solid and fit. It doesn't make a woman any less female. Everybody can and ought to feel far better in their bodies, whether they like to lift loads, dance, swim, or do anything more.

Myth 3: Women Aren't Major areas of strength; usually, They Shouldn't Lift Loads

The Story: Some accept that women are frail and ought to avoid weighty things.

The Truth: This is off-base. Women are imperative in numerous ways. With legitimate training, women can lift loads and become areas of strength. There's really no need to focus on taking care of business or a woman; it's tied in with preparing and practice.

Myth 4: Weightlifting Is Risky for women

The Story: Some say lifting loads isn't okay for women and can hurt them.

Reality: Any game or action can be hazardous on the off chance that it is not done accurately. With legitimate training and care, weightlifting is okay for everybody, men or women. It's fundamental to gain proficiency with the proper method for lifting loads and pay attention to your body.

Myth 5: Women Ought to Do Cardio Activities

The Story: Certain individuals figure women ought to do practices like running or cycling and keep away from loads.

Reality: Cardio practices are excellent, yet they are, by all accounts, not the only thing. Weightlifting has many advantages for the body, including areas of strength and muscles. Thus, Women ought to hit the treadmill and weightlifting for the best well-being.

Myth 6: In the event that Women Quit Weightlifting, Their Muscles Will Transform into Fat

The Story: that's what some trust; assuming women quit lifting loads, the muscles they construct will become fat.

Reality: This isn't the means by which the body works. Muscles and fat are unique. Assuming somebody quits practicing and eats more, they could acquire fat. Yet, powers won't transform into fat.

Myth 7: Weightlifting Influences Richness in women

The Story: Some think that lifting loads can make it difficult for women to have infants.

Reality: This isn't accurate. Standard weightlifting, done correctly, helps a woman's capacity to have kids. Be that as it may, similar to any activity, it's fundamental to pay attention to the body and rest when required.

Myth 8: Women ought to Lift Just Light Loads

The Story: Some say women ought to lift little loads.

The Truth: Women can lift significant burdens as well, very much like men. The weight an individual ought to raise depends on their training rather than on the off chance that they are a man or woman. With training, women can lift significant burdens securely and actually.

For what reason do these fantasies exist?

For quite a while, society has had thoughts regarding what people ought to do. A few ideas are that women ought to remain at home, be delicate, and not do "extreme" things like games. Yet, times are evolving. Women are demonstrating that they can do anything, including weightlifting.

Weightlifting is for everybody. Women shouldn't have faith in these fantasies. If they have any desire to lift loads, they ought to. It's an incredible method for being solid, fit, and sound. Keep in mind that each woman is unique. What's significant is to do what feels reasonable for yourself and not what others say. Being solid and womanlike can remain inseparable. In this way, women, if you need to lift, pull out all the stops!

CHAPTER 2

THE FEMALE PHYSIOLOGY AND STRENGTH TRAINING

Have you at any point asked why people look and feel changed? This is on the grounds that our bodies work in exceptional ways. In this section, we will investigate how a woman's body is fabricated and the way in which it responds to strength training. We will realize the reason why women' bodies are unique and the way in which areas of strength can become solid through lifting loads. Thus, we should take a plunge and comprehend the fabulous association between a woman's body and strength training!

Hormonal differences and their impact on training

Our bodies depend on hormones in many ways. They resemble minuscule couriers that guide various pieces of our bodies. Very much like a traffic cop coordinating vehicles, chemicals assist with directing our body's capabilities. Also, prepare to be blown away. People have various levels of specific chemicals. This is one reason why our bodies act unexpectedly, particularly with regard to training and working out.

Grasping Chemicals

To start with, we should comprehend what chemicals are. Assume you have a controller for your television. At the point when you press a button, the TV knows what to do. In our bodies, chemicals resemble those buttons on the remote. They convey messages to various parts, assisting them with working accurately.

Key Chemicals in Women

1. Estrogen: This is a major one for women. Estrogen assumes a part in numerous things in a woman's body, similar to her month-to-month cycle and keeping areas of strength for bones. It can likewise influence how her muscles develop and recover after working out.

2. Progesterone: This chemical works intimately with estrogen, particularly in the month-to-month cycle. It likewise affects mindset and energy.

3. Testosterone: Stand by; isn't this a male chemical? Indeed, however, women have it, as well, simply in more modest sums. It helps in building muscles and gives energy.

What Chemicals Mean for Preparing

1. Muscle Development: Testosterone is known for assisting muscles with developing. Since men have a more significant amount of it, they frequently develop fortitude quicker. In any case, that doesn't mean women can't construct muscle. They can, and they do! It might require more significant investment and exertion.

2. Recuperation: After an exercise, our muscles need to recuperate. Estrogen can assist with this. It can behave like a safeguard, safeguarding powers and assisting them with mending quickly. This implies that women could return from ruthless exercise faster than men.

3. Energy Levels: Any individual who has felt very drained or very fiery at various times in the month realizes chemicals play a part in energy. Every so often, a woman could feel like she can run a long-distance race. On different days, simply the prospect of activity makes her need to rest. It's all attached to the ascent and fall of chemicals during the month.

4. Fat Capacity: Here's a tomfoolery (or not really fun) truth. Estrogen influences where women store fat. To this end, numerous women notice fat in regions like the hips and thighs. While it tends to be irritating, it's something characteristic. Furthermore, with the appropriate training, women can condition any region of their body.

5. Bone Strength: Women should be cautious about their bone well-being, particularly as they age. Why? In light of estrogen. As women age and have less estrogen, bones can become more fragile. Yet, here's the uplifting news: strength training can assist with making significant areas of strength for bones safeguard against issues from now on.

Training Tips for Women

Pay attention to Your Body: In light of chemicals, women could feel different consistently. It's fundamental to pay attention to your body. Assuming you feel solid and vigorous, go for that problematic exercise. In the event that you feel tired, pick a lighter activity or rest.

Consistency is Critical: Despite the fact that chemicals influence training, the main thing is to be steady. It implies adhering to your daily workout practice, even on days when you won't feel like it.

Try not to Think about it: Everybody's body is exceptional. Since a man could lift heavier loads or fabricate muscle quicker, women can still accomplish their objectives. Center around your excursion and your advancement.

Look for Exhortation: Assuming that you want an explanation about how to prepare, particularly during various times, request help. Mentors or specialists can offer tips and direction.

Chemicals can appear to be interesting, yet they're simply a characteristic piece of our bodies. For women, understanding these chemicals and what they mean for preparing can be intense. Everything revolves around learning and changing. Keep in mind each woman's body is one of a kind. Embrace it, figure it out, and train it with adoration and care. Your body is fit for unimaginable things, chemicals not!

Muscle fiber type distribution and growth potential

Muscles are made up of tiny threads called muscle fibers. These fibers help our muscles move and do their job. Now, not all muscle fibers are the same. They come in different types, and each style has its particular job.

There are mainly two types of muscle fibers:

1. **Slow-twitch fibers:** Think of these as the 'endurance' fibers. They work for a long time but don't have sudden bursts of power. Imagine going on a long walk; it's these fibers that help you keep going.

2. **Fast-twitch fibers:** These are the 'power' fibers. They give a strong and quick force but get tired quickly. Think of sprinting or lifting a heavy box; these fibers jump into action.

Now, when we exercise or train, these fibers can grow and become stronger. But here's the thing: the way they grow depends on the kind of training we do.

If you do activities like long-distance running or cycling, the slow-twitch fibers get the message. They grow and help you do even better in these activities.

On the other hand, if you're into quick activities like sprinting, jumping, or lifting heavy weights, it's the fast-twitch fibers that wake up. They grow and make you more potent in these actions.

Everyone's muscles have both types of fibers. But some people might naturally have more of one kind. That's why some folks might find they're inherently good at running marathons, while others might be great at sprinting.

It's also why training is essential. With the right exercises, you can help your muscle fibers grow and become better at what they do. Whether you want to build endurance or power, understanding your muscle fibers can be your secret tool.

The menstrual cycle and training considerations

Each woman's body goes through an ordinary cycle known as the period. This cycle prepares her body for pregnancy consistently. Regardless of whether a woman needs to become pregnant, she will, in any case, encounter this cycle. Contingent upon where she is in her process, it can influence how she feels and how she ought to move toward her actual training.

Most women' periods keep going around 28 days, by and large. However, other women's cycles may be more limited or longer.

It begins with the principal day of a woman's period and goes until the day preceding her next period. During the initial, not many days, when a woman gets her period, she might encounter death, cramps, or different side effects. This is her body's approach to shedding the covering of the belly in light of the fact that no pregnancy has occurred.

Following the period, the body gears up to let an egg out of one of the ovaries, an occasion known as ovulation. This usually happens around the center of the cycle. Here, a woman is generally ripe, and there's an opportunity for her to get pregnant on the off chance that she has sex.

In the event that a sperm doesn't treat the egg, it separates, and the body begins planning for the following period. During this stage, chemical levels drop, and a few women could encounter premenstrual side effects.

Presently, when we consider actual training, the feminine cycle assumes a part in deciding a woman's energy levels, strength, and even mindset. During the initial not many days of her period, a woman probably won't feel like extreme exercises. She could feel tired, face cramps, or not be in that frame of mind for work out. Nonetheless, a few women find that doing light activities can assist with facilitating feminine distress.

When the period stage is finished, and before ovulation starts, numerous women find that their energy levels rise. They could feel more powerful and more roused to work out. It tends to be a magnificent chance to participate in additional exhausting exercises or take a stab at a new thing.

After ovulation, as the body gets ready for the chance of the following period, energy levels can disappear. A few women could feel more drained or less persuaded to work out. Once more, this is a chance to be delicate with oneself. It's OK to change to lighter activities or even to take a rest day if necessary.

One key important point is that each women's involvement in her monthly cycle is exceptional. What one woman feels during her interaction may be entirely not the same as another. The best methodology is consistently to pay attention to one's body. On the off chance that daily calls for rest, rest. In the event that one more day brings an eruption of energy, use it to its fullest in preparing.

As well as focusing on energy levels, remaining hydrated is pivotal. Drinking water can assist with feminine issues and furthermore support any activity system. It's additionally crucial to wear open-to attire, particularly during exercises. A few women could feel swelled or touchy during their period, so wearing baggy or stretchy garments can make practice more agreeable.

All in all, understanding the monthly cycle and its consequences for the body can assist women with arranging their training all the more. Being on top of one's body and giving it what it needs, be it rest or exercise, is the way to explore and prepare all through the period.

CHAPTER 3

SETTING CLEAR GOALS

Have you at any point begun something new and felt lost inevitably? Like starting another book, however, getting exhausted halfway in light of the fact that you want to sort out where the story's going? That is the very thing that plunging into strength training can feel like without clear objectives. Envision objectives as the thrilling plot focuses on your wellness story, motivating each step you take. In this section, we'll talk about why understanding what you need from your exercises is imperative. We'll dive into the core of what drives you, making each drop of sweat count. Each push, pull, and lift in the exercise center has a more profound significance when attached to a reasonable reason. Thus, we should sort out yours together!

Defining your purpose aesthetic, health, performance

Beginning a fitness venture is similar to sowing a seed. For it to develop and prosper, it requires consistent consideration, a suitable climate, and, fundamentally, an unmistakable vision of what the developed plant ought to resemble. Likewise, understanding your 'why' behind plunging into the universe of fitness can be the directing star that lights up your way.

Individuals frequently float towards three essential reasons when they choose to set out on this excursion: style, well-being, and execution. We should jump further into each.

Tasteful Objectives

For the majority, the visual aftereffects of their diligent effort become the inspiration. They're driven by the fantasy of chiseled arms, a conditioned midsection, or legs that have seen miles of running and long periods of squats. Our general surroundings, including films, magazines, and online entertainment, frequently stress feelings, making it a well-known inspiration.

However, the excursion towards tasteful objectives is profoundly private. One individual's ideal body type can contrast incomprehensibly with another's. Subsequently, pursuing a stylish dream implies routinely checking in with oneself, guaranteeing that the pursuit comes from self-esteem and not cultural strain. Creating a plan for yourself causes you to feel glad, sure, and cheerful.

In any case, it's vital that while feelings can be propelling, they ought not to be the sole justification for one's wellness process. Alone, they won't offer the food required for the long stretch.

Well-being Objectives

Another significant motivation behind why many dig into fitness is to help their well-being. For some purposes, this could mean shedding a few additional pounds to keep illnesses under control. At the same time, for other people, it may be tied in with reinforcing the heart, further developing lung limits, or guaranteeing better bone thickness as they age.

Zeroing in on well-being implies understanding the bunch of ways practice helps the body past precisely what it looks like. Incessant work-out has been displayed to bring down the gamble of persistent sicknesses, work on emotional well-being, increment life expectancy, and upgrade and sizeable personal satisfaction. For individuals who have confronted medical problems or have seen friends and family wrestle with them, zeroing in on well-being becomes central.

At the point when well-being is the main thrust, the triumphs are in inches lost or muscle acquired as well as in cholesterol levels dropping, pulse balancing out, and sugars remaining under wraps.

Execution Objectives

Then there are those determined by the sheer rush of what their bodies can accomplish. They're not simply hoping to look great or lighthearted; they're pursuing the high of execution. Could I run a mile in less than 6 minutes? Will I dead lift two times my body weight? Could I, at any point, overcome that complex yoga present? For their purposes, the exercise center or the running track turns into a jungle gym to test their cutoff points.

Execution-driven wellness devotees frequently set clear benchmarks for themselves. They may be making progress toward running a long-distance race, contending in a weightlifting rivalry, or completing a marathon. Their training is explicitly custom-made to improve their abilities and lift their presentation in their picked region.

Their triumphs are estimated in private outclasses, in the excitement of crossing an end goal or dominating a method they've been dealing with for a really long time. The delight of execution lies in the excursion, the discipline, the commitment, and the sheer resolution it takes to stretch one's body to its most extreme boundaries.

The universe of wellness is immense, with various ways to step. Whether feeling, well-being, or execution drives one, the critical lies in understanding and recognizing that reason. Each course, while different, offers its delights and difficulties.

Yet, regardless of the way picked, it's crucial to approach it with deference for one's body, grasping its necessities, and showing restraint. It's similarly indispensable to recollect that one's motivation could develop. Somebody who begins for tasteful reasons could track down euphoria in execution or value the medical advantages they gather.

At last, the fitness venture is a profoundly private one, a settlement between you and your body. Anything the explanation you decide to leave on this excursion, let it give pleasure, satisfaction, and a feeling of achievement. Your motivation is your own, and it's commendable, regardless of what it is.

The importance of realistic goal setting

Life is filled up with desires, dreams, and goals. As we move through our excursion, defining objectives becomes fundamental for guiding our longings. Nonetheless, it's not just about setting any intention; it's tied in with laying out reasonable goals. Understanding and valuing the meaning of affordable objective setting can have a significant effect on our accomplishments and mental prosperity.

Laying out objectives is like finding an area on a guide. In the event that you pick a site excessively far and with restricted assets, you may never arrive at it. Notwithstanding, assuming you choose a spot that is testing yet feasible with your assistance, the excursion becomes pleasant and satisfying.

At the point when we discuss sensible objectives, it's tied in with offsetting desire with feasibility. Everybody has wants; however, establishing these cravings in reality is critical. For example, while it's commendable to intend to turn into a long-distance runner, hoping to accomplish this accomplishment in seven days in the event that you've never run before is unreasonable.

All in all, why is defining reasonable objectives so significant? It, first and foremost, forms certainty. Each time you accomplish a fantasy, it builds up your faith in your capacities. It's an approval that you can focus intently on something and achieve it. Then again, consistently neglecting to meet ridiculous objectives can dissolve fearlessness and breed insecurities.

Another tremendous perspective is inspiration. Accomplishing objectives gives a feeling of fulfillment. Each time you arrive at a goal, it powers the motivation to seek after the following one. At the point when objectives are excessively elevated and remain neglected, it isn't very encouraging. The underlying excitement disappears, and the whole undertaking can begin feeling silly.

Besides, reasonable objectives guarantee the ideal utilization of assets, essentially investment. These are limited and important. Unreasonable dreams can lead you down ways that consume these assets without yielding outcomes, causing dissatisfaction and burnout.

Even with aspiration, existence can be sub-par. There's a slender line between testing yourself and defining ridiculous objectives. Excessively aggressive goals can prompt depletion and frustration. On the off chance that you're ceaselessly in a condition of endeavoring without accomplishing, it's intellectually depleting. Over the long haul, it can encourage negative self-insights and even lead to hurtful ways of behaving, particularly assuming you're attempting to pursue faster routes to accomplish these excessively aggressive objectives.

Things being what they are, how might one figure out some harmony and put forth reasonable objectives? Begin with an intensive self-evaluation. Know where you stand concerning the arrangement. You're holding back nothing. In the event that it's an expertise, evaluate your ongoing capability. In the event that it's a wellness target, assess your present state of being. When you have a reasonable comprehension of your beginning stage, you can diagram a way ahead.

Exploration can likewise assist with establishing your objectives in actuality. Gain from the encounters of others. On the off chance that you're wandering into another business, concentrate on the company and figure out the development directions of comparable organizations. On the off chance that it's a self-improvement objective, read about others' excursions.

Besides, recollect that accomplishing a giant objective is an interaction, not an occasion. Separate the bigger target into more modest undertakings or achievements. Each accomplished achievement can be a wellspring of inspiration to handle the following.

Finally, putting forth an objective is definitely not a one-time act. It's essential to survey your dreams intermittently. This reflection permits you to celebrate accomplishments, grasp barricades, and change your methodology if vital.

Eventually, the objective setting is profoundly private. It's an impression of one's desires, wants, and yearnings. While it's vital to think ambitiously, it's similarly critical to guarantee that these fantasies are established in actuality. Defining reasonable objectives offers a guide to progress, ensuring that the excursion is as remunerating as the objective.

CHAPTER 4

ESSENTIAL EQUIPMENT AND GYM FAMILIARITY

Imagine walking into a kitchen for the first time. The ovens, broilers, and utensils are overpowering on the off chance that you don't know what each is for. An exercise center can be a labyrinth of machines, loads, and gear for newbie's. Be that as it may, with a touch of direction, what once appeared to be scary can turn into your jungle gym. In this section, we'll demystify the exercise center, acquainting you with fundamental gear and assisting you with exploring this space with certainty. Whether you're a carefully prepared exercise center participant searching for a boost or venturing onto the exercise center floor interestingly, understanding the devices available to you can raise your exercise insight.

Home gym vs. commercial gym: Pros and Cons

The choice of where to work it out — whether in the comfort of your home or inside the stimulating walls of a business exercise center — frequently reduces to individual inclinations. The two choices accompany their benefits and downsides. To help you settle on a wise decision, we should thoroughly look at the benefits and burdens of both home exercise centers and business exercise centers.

Home Exercise center

Pros

1. Comfort: The accommodation that a home rec center gives is its most colossal benefit. There's a compelling reason to drive, saving you both time and the problem of engaging traffic or public transportation. Step into your exercise space, and you're all set.

2. Adaptability: With a home rec center, you're not limited by functional hours. Do you want to work out at noon or first light? Forget about it. Your rec center is dependably open.

3. Protection: For some, the capacity to work out without feeling noticed or judged is significant. At home, you can practice without feeling unsure, permitting you to zero in entirely on your daily schedule.

4. **Cost-Effective in the Long Run**: Albeit the underlying venture can be substantial, over the long run, a home exercise center can demonstrate more savvy. There are no everyday participation expenses, and you purchase just the gear that suits your requirements.

5. Customization: Your home rec center can be custom-made to your inclinations. Whether it's the sort of hardware, the music, or the stylistic layout, you have unlimited authority over the climate.

Cons

1. Introductory Expense: A critical starting venture is essential to set up a home exercise center, particularly in the event that you need a choice of excellent gear.

2. Space Necessities: Some have the advantage of extra space. Designating a committed region for rec center hardware in more modest homes can be a challenge.

3. Restricted Hardware: You should have an enormous financial plan and more than adequate space to manage with restricted gear, confining the range of activities you can do.

4. Absence of Social Collaboration: Working out at home can be desolate. You pass up the fellowship and inspiration that comes from a bunch of exercises or just being around other wellness fans.

5. Potential for Interruptions: At home, you're encircled by expected interruptions, whether it's family tasks, relatives, or that enticing sofa.

Commercial Gym

Pros

1. Assortment of Hardware: Commercial Gym exercise centers offer a wide variety of gear, taking special care of a wide range of exercises — from strength training to cardio and particular classes.

2. Inspiring Air: Being encircled by individuals devoted to their wellness objectives can be an immense inspiration supporter. The energy in a business exercise center is frequently irresistible.

3. Proficient Direction: Most business rec centers have coaches close by. On the off chance that you're new to working out or require direction, this expert help can be significant.

4. Social Communication: Rec centers can be incredible spots to mingle and meet similar people. Bunch classes, specifically, can encourage a feeling of the local area.

5. Extra Conveniences: Numerous business rec centers offer added conveniences like saunas, pools, or back rub administrations, upgrading the general wellness experience.

Cons

1. Cost: Participation charges, particularly for top-of-the-line rec centers, can be intense. Furthermore, there are many times additional expenses for individual training or particular classes.

2. Travel Time: Driving to the exercise center can, once in a while, be an impediment, particularly on the off chance that it's far from your home or work environment.

3. Stand by Times: Well-known exercise centers can become busy during top hours, meaning you could need to sit tight for your chance on unambiguous hardware.

4. Less Customized: While you can pick your daily schedule, the climate — music, stylistic layout, lighting — is set by the rec center, ruling out private inclinations.

5. Functional Hours: Most rec centers have set timings. On the off chance that you're an evening person or a go-getter, these hours could, in some cases, line up with your favored exercise times.

Choosing between a Commercial Gym center and a home rec center includes weighing individual inclinations, spending plans, and long-haul wellness objectives. Some could flourish in the energetic energy of a clamoring rec center, while others lean toward the isolation and comfort of home exercises. It's fundamental to pick a climate where you feel spurred and can stay reliable in your wellness process. The best exercise center is the one you'll really utilize.

Must-have equipment for effective training

A well-equipped gym, be it at home or business, can fundamentally upgrade the viability of exercises. The suitable devices offer flexibility as well as guarantee that activities are performed securely and proficiently. Here is a rundown of must-have hardware for pragmatic training, taking special care of the two fledglings and prepared wellness fans.

1. Hand weights

Hand weights are the most adaptable bits of hardware. They are ideal for compound developments like squats, thrusts, and presses, as well as separation activities, for example, bicep twists or rear arm muscle augmentations. Accessible in different loads, they consider moderate over-burden, which is critical for nonstop improvement.

2. Obstruction Groups

Lightweight and versatile opposition groups are priceless, particularly for the people who travel often. They give obstruction during strength practices and can be utilized for various exercises focusing on different muscle gatherings. They're additionally astounding for restoration practices and further developing adaptability.

3. Hand Weight Set

Hand weights, similar to hand weights, are crucial for strength training. They're fundamental for compound developments like dead lifts, seat presses, and squats. Putting resources into a customizable hand weight set guarantees, you can gradually increment weight as you progress.

4. Pull-Up Bar

Pull-ups are a far-reaching exercise that objectives the chest area, including the back, shoulders, and arms. A draw-up bar, frequently introduced in entryways or walls, is a smaller gear piece that works with this compound development. For those incapable of doing a full draw-up at first, opposition groups can be utilized for help.

5. Weight Seat

A weight seat is fundamental for practices like seat presses, rear arm muscle plunges, and step-ups. A movable bar, which can be set at different grades and declines, offers greater flexibility, empowering a more extensive scope of activities.

6. Iron weights

Iron weights are unique as they consolidate cardiovascular, strength, and adaptability training. Practices like portable weight swings, cup squats, or Turkish outfits can be proficient for full-body exercises.

7. Dependability Ball (Swiss Ball)

Dependability balls are incredible for center activities and further developing equilibrium and stance. They can likewise act as a seat elective for explicit weight works out, expanding the test by presenting a component of precariousness.

8. Hop open

Working out with rope is a fantastic, high-impact exercise that additionally further develops timing, agility, and coordination. It's a staple for some competitors, particularly fighters. However, anybody can profit from the full-body movement a leap rope gives.

9. Medication Ball

Medication balls are weighted circles that can enhance many activities. They can be utilized for strength training, ply metrics, or center exercises. Throwing, lifting, or involving them as opposition can add tests to schedules.

10. Froth Roller

While not straightforwardly an exercise instrument, froth rollers are fundamental for recovery. They help in my of ascial discharge, facilitating muscle snugness, further developing the bloodstream, and supporting muscle fixes. Consistently utilizing a froth roller can improve adaptability and reduce the gamble of wounds.

11. Yoga Mat

Regardless of whether you're not into yoga, a decent mat is valuable for floor activities, extending, and center exercises.

They give padding and grasp, guaranteeing solace and security during workouts.

12. Treadmill or Exercise Bike

For those zeroing in on cardiovascular wellbeing, having a treadmill or exercise bike can be significant, particularly during unfriendly weather patterns. Current adaptations frequently accompany preset projects, following abilities, and opposition settings to shift exercise forces.

13. Power Rack or Squat Rack

For extreme weightlifters, a power or squat rack is a commendable venture. It guarantees that activities like squats or weighty hand weight lifts are performed securely, particularly assuming one is working out without a spotter.

While the above gear pieces are considered fundamental for a balanced training outline, the best hardware must be the one that lines up with your wellness objectives. You can skip each part of the start or keep a compelling gym routine daily practice. Novices can begin with fundamental gear and, bit by bit, add to their assortment as they progress.

Eventually, while gear can upgrade exercises, assurance, consistency, and a very arranged routine are the central components of commonsense training. Whether you're sorting out in a space loaded up with the most recent gadgets or in a moderate setting, the vital lies in the way you use what's accessible to accomplish your wellness goals.

CHAPTER 5

CORE STRENGTH TRAINING PRINCIPLES

Recollect when you previously figured out how to ride a bicycle. Recall the wobbles, the vulnerability, and afterward, that elating second when you at last tracked down your offset and accelerated forward with sheer happiness? Strength training has a comparative bend. At its heart, it isn't just about raising loads or pursuing muscle definition; it's a dance of figuring out your body, its cutoff points, and the science behind each flex and stretch. In this part, we'll return to the rudiments, similar to returning to that old bicycle ride memory. We'll investigate the primary standards of strength training, according to a course book point of view, yet by interfacing them with our regular encounters and senses. It's an excursion of revelation, understanding, and, in particular, associating with the actual embodiment of what makes strength training extraordinary.

Progressive overload explained

In the realm of strength training and fitness, assuming there's a rule that goes the distance and examination, it's dynamic overburden. Similar to dominating an instrument or a language, the thought rotates around slow movement. You couldn't anticipate playing Beethoven in your most memorable piano example, correct? Essentially, lifting loads and developing fortitude requires an efficient expansion in power to proceed with headway.

Moderate over-burden is the act of constantly expanding the requests on the outer muscle framework to continue to develop muscle, strength, and perseverance. However, to get more grounded and fitter, you should reliably make your muscles work harder than they're utilized to. Assuming you do similar activities with similar weight and reiterations like clockwork, your body adjusts and quits moving along.

At its center, the rationale is instinctive: as your body changes with a test, the specific undertaking turns out to be more open. Thus, to keep creating, you'll have to raise the stakes a little, be it through weight, redundancies, or power. At the point when muscles face opposition, minuscule tears happen. Yet, don't be frightened; this is a characteristic piece of muscle development. As these small tears fix, the muscle remakes more considerably than previously, setting itself up for the expanded requests you'll put on it.

In any case, while the rule is direct, its application requires cautious thought. It's enticing to feel that assuming some opposition is great, more should be better. Be that as it may, such as overwatering a plant in the expectation it'll become quicker, an excess of too early can blow up. Overburdening without giving the body satisfactory opportunity to recuperate can prompt wounds.

Yet, how would you rehearse moderate overburden without getting carried away? It's about balance. Begin by somewhat expanding the weight you're lifting, however, just when your ongoing weight feels reasonable. In the event that you want additional opportunities to prepare for a weight bounce, think about expanding the quantity of reiterations or sets. Another technique is to change the speed of your redundancies or lessen the rest time between sets.

Nonetheless, featuring the significance of paying attention to your body is fundamental. Sharp agonies, joint distress, or delayed irritation may be pointers that you're advancing excessively fast or utilizing an ill-advised structure. Besides, while the standard of moderate over-burden is focal, recuperation is its quiet accomplice. Each time you challenge your muscles, sufficient rest and nourishment are indispensable for them to fix, develop, and return more grounded.

In numerous ways, moderate over-burden reflects life's more extensive examples. It advises us that development isn't about terrific jumps but steady, gradual endeavors. While the loads, reps, and sets are substantial measurements, the basic example is general: challenge, adjust, develop, and rehash. Whether you're lifting a hand weight, running a mile, or dominating another expertise, the excursion of movement is a dance of persistence, constancy, and stretching the limits barely to the point of starting development.

Importance of rest and recovery

Chasing actual physical fitness, many could invoke pictures of challenging exercises, sweat-doused clothing, and the refreshing weariness that follows a problematic instructional meeting. However, there's a frequently disregarded side to this excursion: rest and Recuperation. Similarly, as night follows day, the body's requirement for mending is as pivotal as the work put into each rep, lap, or jump.

The Physiology of Recuperation

To really see the value in the significance of rest, one should dive into the physiology of activity. At the point when we participate in active work, particularly extreme focus exercises or strength training, we make minuscule tears in our muscles. This is definitely not something terrible. As a matter of fact, it's a characteristic cycle by which the body remakes these tears, making the muscles more powerful than previously, a peculiarity called muscle hypertrophy.

Additionally, the body goes through its stores of glycogen, the essential energy hotspot for muscles, during exercise. The body additionally aggregates metabolic byproducts like lactic corrosive, which can weaken muscle capability and add to irritation.

Recuperation permits the body to reestablish glycogen stores, fix muscle tissue, and kill these side effects. Without satisfactory rest, muscles stay in this, to some degree harmed, drained state, which can prompt overtraining and the potential for wounds.

Actual Advantages of Appropriate Recuperation

1. Muscle Development: As referenced previously, muscle fortifying happens not during the exercise but rather in the recuperation period. On the off chance that we continually separate our muscles without allowing them to fix, we pass up the real advantages of preparing.

2. Counteraction of Overtraining Disorder: Overtraining is an extreme and regular peculiarity. It can prompt ongoing weariness, a decline in execution, expanded hazard of wounds, and other medical problems.

3. Diminished Hazard of Wounds: Ceaseless mileage without legitimate Recuperation can compound muscle strains and tendon injuries and lead to ongoing joint agony.

4. Ideal Resistant Capability: In workaholic behavior, the body, without sufficient rest, can think twice about the invulnerable framework, making us more powerless against sicknesses.

Mental and Mental Advantages

Rest isn't just about actual prosperity; it's similarly fundamental for psychological well-being.

1. Counteraction of Burnout: Similarly, as muscles weaken without Recuperation, the psyche can likewise become depleted, prompting an absence of inspiration, diminished energy, and potential burnout.

2. Further developed Rest Quality: Customary activity, joined with sufficient Recuperation, frequently brings about better rest designs, which further upgrade the body's capacity to fix and develop.

3. Mental Lucidity and Concentration: Ceaseless training without breaks can prompt mental exhaustion. Recuperation periods can assist with restoring the psyche, guaranteeing better focus during exercises.

Dynamic versus Aloof Recuperation

Recuperation here and there means accomplishing some different option from doing literally nothing. There's a differentiation between uninvolved and dynamic Recuperation.

Aloof Recuperation alludes to finishing rest with no active work. It's tied in with allowing your body to recuperate with no effort, which is, in some cases, fundamental, particularly after profoundly overwhelming exercises or contests.

Dynamic Recuperation, By and by, just low-power movement, low-influence exercises like strolling, cycling, or yoga. Such activities can advance the bloodstream without overburdening the muscles, helping in the evacuation of metabolic waste and conveying supplements fundamental for fixing.

A Critical Support Point in Recuperation

Recovery isn't exclusively about what you do or don't do regarding actual work. Nourishment assumes an essential part. Consuming legitimate supplements, particularly not long after an exercise, can fundamentally influence the recuperation interaction.

Proteins are imperative for muscle fixing, while sugars assist with recharging glycogen stores. Hydration is similarly urgent, as exercises lead to liquid misfortune through sweat. Supplanting these liquids helps in supplement transport and can forestall muscle issues and fits.

In the ensemble of wellness, rest, and Recuperation are the stops between the notes that give the song its magnificence and profundity. They are not interferences to the excursion but rather fundamental parts that shape and characterize it.

It's a comprehensive circle of effort and unwinding. The work pushes the limits, and the harmony merges the increases, setting up the body and psyche for the following test. Perceiving the significance of rest and Recuperation is a demonstration of figuring out one's body, regarding its signs, and focusing on an excursion of well-being and prosperity in its most genuine sense. Wellness isn't a run but a long-distance race, where the excursion's maintainability is essentially as pivotal as the outcomes.

Balancing volume and intensity

Exploring the fitness scene can frequently outline a course through a vast, complicated labyrinth. Key to this excursion is two vital boundaries: volume and force. Both assume crucial parts in molding your training results, and understanding how to control them is central to progress.

Volume, at its center, exemplifies the aggregate sum of work you do during your exercises. In the event that you're a weightlifter, this means the quantity of sets and redundancies you complete. For a long-distance runner, volume implies the miles signed in seven days. Power, then again, digs into how hard you propel yourself during these exercises. With regards to lifting, it's about the load on the bar. For a sprinter, it's the speed kept up with during those miles.

The connection between volume and power is perplexing and frequently contrarily corresponding. At the point when you push hard as far as power, the book regularly should be directed to stay away from overexertion, as well as the other way around. It's suggestive of adjusting on a tightrope; resting a lot on one side without remunerating can prompt a fall or, in wellness terms, wounds or burnout.

High-volume, low-power training regimens are perseverance manufacturers. They condition the muscles to support delayed action, which is ideal for competitors like marathon runners or cyclists. This approach likewise offers the additional benefit of refining strategy. For novices particularly, redundancy at lower powers assists in dominating with shaping, establishing a groundwork for future movement. Besides, meetings of lower power act as dynamic recuperation. They animate blood stream to the muscles without excessively burdening them, advancing, mending, and fixing.

Alternately, when the spotlight is on extreme focus with decreased volume, the objectives shift towards creating strength and power. This approach reverberates with runners, weightlifters, or anybody hoping to fabricate muscle rapidly. Focused energy meetings are proficient; they guarantee significant additions in a dense period. Exercises like Intense cardio exercise (HIIT) additionally stir up the metabolic fire, ensuring that you consume calories even during the training.

Be that as it may, how can one find some harmony between these two?

Understanding your goals is the beginning stage. Your training ought to mirror your objectives. In the event that building endurance is needed, incline towards higher volume. Assuming that crude power or muscle development best the rundown, force ought to become the dominant focal point.

Per iodization offers another point of view. It's the act of consistently changing volume and power. There may be weeks or months where the emphasis is on sloping up the book, step by step, moving to stages where power turns into the essential driver.

In any case, in the midst of this specialized shuffle, the significance of tuning into your body's signs couldn't possibly be more significant. In the event that there's determined weariness or assuming exercises become a feared errand, it very well may be an ideal opportunity to rethink. The volume may be excessively burdening, or the power isn't lined up with current abilities. Alternately, assuming activities feel excessively easy it may be a pointer to challenge you further.

Recovery is one more aspect of this conversation. Serious meetings request more personal time for the body to recover. It's during these rest periods that the enchantment occurs: muscles revamp, becoming more grounded and more muscular. Thus, as it were, recuperation turns into the quiet accomplice to volume and power, meriting equivalent consideration.

Finally, there's no mischief in looking for direction. Mentors, coaches, or prepared competitors can offer significant experiences, guaranteeing you stay focused. They can assist with fitting an arrangement that weds volume and force agreeably, redid to your novel requirements.

The dance between volume and force is liquid and constantly advancing. Like a culinary expert changing fixings to consummate a dish, finding the right mix of these training parts is both an artistry and a science. It requires persistence, reflection, and, now and then, a sprinkle of experimentation. Be that as it may, when done well, the outcomes can be extraordinary, driving you towards your wellness goals with energy.

CHAPTER 6

FORM AND TECHNIQUE MASTERY

Plunge into any art, and you'll before long understand that the brightness frequently lies in the subtleties. In the domain of fitness and strength training, this splendor is exemplified by structure and strategy. While the loads we lift and the miles we catch the spotlight, the nuances of our developments organize the genuine ensemble of progress. Appropriate structure isn't just about looking great or mimicking the experts; it's the foundation of proficiency, the safeguard against wounds, and the compass that coordinates each step toward its objective. In this part, we'll disentangle the subtleties of structure and strategy, stressing why dominating them isn't simply suggested but fundamental. Whether you're making your most memorable strides in the wellness venture or have miles behind you, understanding and idealizing your structure can be the unique advantage you've been searching for.

Why correct form matters

You've recently strolled into a rec center, new tennis shoes on, playlist prepared, and inspiration at its pinnacle. You've seen recordings of individuals lifting loads, and you're anxious to make a plunge. In any case, stand by! Before you snatch those loads, there's an essential thing to consider - the specialty of the proper structure.

Similarly, as you would only begin driving with knowing the guidelines of the street, jumping carelessly into practices without understanding legitimate structure can be a recipe for difficulties. What difference does it make to such an extent? How about we separate it?

First and foremost, everything revolves around proficiency. The proper structure guarantees that you're focusing on the suitable muscle bunches during explicit activities. Have you heard somebody say they didn't "feel" an activity where they should? Frequently, this is on the grounds that their structure was off. Appropriate method guarantees that each squat, lift, or lurch does what it should, raising a ruckus around town muscles and giving you all the more value for your money. It resembles singing on key; in addition to the fact that it sounds better, it likewise guarantees the tune conveys its expected inclination.

Security is one more gigantic piece of the situation. The wrong structure is a one-way pass to Strongsville and Sprains town. With the correct method, you're putting excessive weight on fragments of the body that are prepared to deal with it. Think about it like attempting to utilize a spoon to cut a steak — it's simply not the right instrument to make it happen. Safeguarding your joints, ligaments, and muscles by using the proper structure can be the contrast between a compensating exercise and weeks (or even months) spent uninvolved.

And afterward, there's progress. Assuming you're hoping to improve — whether it's lifting heavier, running quicker, or it is critical to bounce higher — consistency. In any case, it's difficult to be steady, assuming you're often nursing wounds from mistaken structure. Likewise, as you get more grounded and fitter, the appropriate method takes into consideration more exact following of progress. It's more straightforward to quantify improvement when factors (like structure) stay consistent.

Ultimately, it's tied in with building a solid groundwork. Positive routines, once settled, are challenging to break. By imbuing the proper structure all along, you're getting yourself in a position for a smoother wellness venture. It turns out to be natural, such as tying your shoestrings or cleaning your teeth, and on the other side, forgetting persistent vices. That is an intense treatment and frequently more testing than advancing the correct way at every turn.

All in all, while the load on the free weight or the speed on the treadmill could seem like the superstars, the uncelebrated yet truly great individual is, without a doubt, structure. It supports each move, guaranteeing proficiency, security, and consistent advancement. Thus, whenever you're going to set out on an exercise, pause for a minute to check in with your structure. A little step guarantees enormous prizes. In the ensemble of wellness, design sets the musicality, and with the right beat, you're dependably on target to raise a ruckus around town notes.

Tips for common exercises like squats, dead lifts, and presses

In the cosmic system of strength training, certain activities are hailed as foundations, framing the groundwork of numerous fitness regimens. Among these, squats, dead lifts, and squeezes hold an exceptional spot. When executed with accuracy, these activities can open an orchestra of strength and muscle improvement. Nonetheless, making a plunge without understanding their complexities can prompt disappointing outcomes or, more terrible, wounds. We should dig into these activities, offering a compass to direct you through their subtleties.

Squats: The Lord of Lower Body Work

OK, the squat! Venerated by quite a few people, a compound development basically focuses on the quadriceps, hamstrings, and gluts yet additionally draws in the center and lowers back.

• **Foot Arrangement:** Begin with feet shoulder-width separated. Slight varieties are OK in view of solace. However, this is a decent guideline.

- **Profundity Matters:** Plan to go as low as your versatility permits, preferably until thighs are lined up with the ground or more profound. This profundity guarantees the most significant muscle commitment.

- **Keep the Chest Up:** As you plunge, keep your chest lifted and back unbiased. Envision wearing an ID on your shirt and attempting to show it off all through the development.

- **Pass Through Heels:** As you push back up, consider driving the energy through your heels, guaranteeing stable ground contact and ideal power creation.

Deadlifts: A Definitive Power Move

The dead lift, frequently named the most basic of lifts, makes all the difference for the back chain, including the hamstrings, gluts, and whole back.

- **Grasp and Position:** Stand with feet hip-width separated. Grasp the bar right against your knees. You can utilize a twofold overhand grasp or a blended hold, with one hand looking towards you and the other confronting endlessly.

- **Lift with Your Hips and Legs**: While it could appear to be a chest area development, the force of the dead lift comes from your hips and legs. Start by pushing through the ground, broadening your hips and knees all the while.

- **Nonpartisan Spine is Vital:** From your neck down to your tailbone, it is essential to keep an impartial spine. Consider holding a pencil between your shoulder bones and keeping a twofold jaw all through the development.

- **Bar Way:** The bar ought to go in a straight upward line. It ought to remain near your body, brushing against your shins and thighs.

Presses: Chiseling the Chest area

Whether it's the above press for shoulders or the seat press for the chest, squeezing developments are quintessential for chest area improvement.

- **Hold**: For seat presses, a grasp marginally more extensive than shoulder width is average. For the above squeezes, situating hands right external the shoulders is average. Guarantee even hold and equivalent strain in two hands.

- **Stable Establishment:** No matter what the press type, security in the lower body is critical. In a seat press, this implies driving your feet into the ground and crushing your gluts. The above squeezes include a propped center and established feet.

- **Way and Elbow Position**: In the seat press, as you bring down the bar, elbows ought to shape a 45-degree point with the middle. The bar contacts the lower chest, and you push it back up in a slight bend. For the above squeezes, keep the elbows somewhat before the hand weight during the underlying stage, pushing the bar straight up while moving the head somewhat back.

- **Connect with the Center: Particularly** in the above presses, a tight center forestalls excessive curving of the back, guaranteeing well-being and power transmission from the beginning.

Consolidating these Tips

In light of these fundamental signs, it's memorable fundamental that careful discipline brings about promising results. While first zeroing in on the structure, utilizing lighter weights is astute. Along these lines, you can fabricate muscle memory without unreasonable strain. As you become more capable, step-by-step expanding the weight guarantees you receive the strength and hypertrophy rewards of these activities.

Also, consider getting criticism. Whether it's from a confirmed mentor or recording yourself to investigate later, outer information can pinpoint regions you could neglect.

Shutting Considerations

Squats, dead lifts, and presses resemble the three mainstays of an old sanctuary, each supporting the design of a balanced wellness schedule. Nonetheless, their adequacy is enhanced when performed with appropriate strategy. In the realm of wellness, it's about the excursion or the objective as well as about how you explore the way. With the proper structure and careful execution, you're nearer to your goals, as well as guaranteeing an excursion that is protected, productive, and significantly fulfilling.

CHAPTER 7

BUILDING A SOLID FOUNDATION – THE BEGINNER'S PLAN

Recollect the excitement of riding a bicycle, interestingly? The unbalanced beginnings, the momentary snapshots of equilibrium, and afterward, the refreshing sensation of the breeze against your face as you, at last, accelerated forward all alone? Start a fitness journey inspires a comparable mixed drink of feelings: energy, vulnerability, assurance, and happiness. Similar to how you would only leave on a long bicycle ride with first dominating the fundamentals, plunging profoundly into fitness requires significant areas of strength for balance. This chapter isn't just about sets, reps, or schedules; it's tied in with embracing the delightful starting points, understanding the 'whys' behind the 'how,' and building a relationship with your body. We should set out on this excursion together, clasping hands as you move into the tremendous, remunerating universe of fitness.

Compound movements

Assuming the universe of strength training was an ensemble, compound developments would be its most thunderous orchestras. These activities, celebrated for their complex advantages, have become the essence of numerous workout regimes, from amateur to tip-top. However, what makes them so exceptional, and why have they procured such love in the wellness local area?

At the center, compound movements are practices that draw in different muscle gatherings and joints all the while. They stand rather than seclusion works out, which focus on a solitary muscle bunch and include development around one joint. The thing that matters is similar to preparing a whole feast as opposed to planning only one dish; both have their benefits. However, the previous offers a more extravagant, more comprehensive experience.

Take the exemplary dead lift, for instance. While it principally focuses on the muscles of the back chain, including the gluts, hamstrings, and lower back, it likewise needs support from the center, lower arms, and, surprisingly, the last. It's a full-body try, requesting coordination, strength, and equilibrium.

Anyway, why are compound movements hailed as the bedrock of viable training?

Efficiency: In the present speedy world, many are in a hurry. Compound movements offer an answer, working different muscle bunches in a solitary activity. Rather than moving to start with one machine and then onto the next, focusing on individual muscles, practices like squats, seat presses, or pull-ups give far-reaching exercises in a more limited period.

Functional Strength: Day-to-day exercises, is it lifting a crate, playing with children, or planting, require the synergistic activity of numerous muscles. Compound movements mirror these genuine movements, improving functional strength and making ordinary undertakings more straightforward.

Calorie Consume: Due to their multi-joint nature, these activities require more energy. This means more fatty consumption during the exercise and, surprisingly, a raised metabolic rate post-workout.

Balance and Coordination: Executing compound activities requires a specific degree of equilibrium and coordination, advancing muscular strength as well as neuromuscular capability.

Hormonal Advantages: Activities that include huge muscle bunches have been displayed to evoke a more critical hormonal reaction, especially with regard to the development of chemicals and testosterone, both essential for muscle development and recovery.

Flexibility and Versatility: While it could appear to be unreasonable when performed with legitimate strategy and full scope of movement, many compound developments can upgrade adaptability and joint portability.

In light of these benefits, we should highlight a couple of quintessential compound activities:

- **Squats:** Frequently eluded to as the ruler of activities, squats dominatingly focus on the quadriceps, hamstrings, and gluts. In any case, they likewise draw in the center, back, and, surprisingly, the calves. Whether with body weight or added obstruction, squats are an essential development for leg strength and, by and large, usefulness.

- **Seat Press:** This exemplary chest area practice focuses on the chest yet, in addition, draws in the rear arm muscles and shoulders. The adjustment expected during the press additionally implies the center and back muscles become an integral factor.

- **Pull-Ups/Jaw Ups:** While they focus on the back muscles (especially the last), these pulling practices additionally work the biceps, shoulders, and center.

- **Lines:** Be it free weight columns, hand weight lines, or machine pushes, this pulling movement reinforces the back, biceps, and shoulders, with the center giving adjustment.

- **Above Press:** This pushing development centers around the shoulders yet additionally includes the rear arm muscles, upper chest, and, while standing, even the center and legs for adjustment.

Leaving on compound developments can be threatening right away. There's a ton to consider: structure, breathing, equilibrium, and coordination. However, similar to learning another dialect, with training, these activities become natural. The words transform into sentences, sentences into passages, and in no time, you're quickly talking in the rich language of wellness.

For those new to these developments, beginning with lighter loads or even body weight is fitting. As capability develops, obstruction can be gradually expanded, guaranteeing reliable advancement without compromising well-being.

All in all, compound movements are something other than works out; they're a festival of what the human body can accomplish. They advise us that in solidarity, there is strength, and when muscles work together as one, the outcomes are absolutely musical. Whether you're a novice making the primary strides or an accomplished competitor refining your specialty, embracing compound developments guarantees an excursion of growth, strength, and all-encompassing prosperity. Top of Form

A sample 8-week beginner's strength training program

Stepping into the universe of strength training can be both invigorating and overpowering. Knowing where to start may be troublesome on the grounds that there are countless activities, strategies, and schedules accessible. In any case, similar to any lengthy excursion, the initial step is frequently the most pivotal. This 8-week program is intended for novices, accentuating the primary parts of strength training while at the same time guaranteeing consistent movement.

Weeks 1-2: Establishing the Foundation

Goal: Familiarize yourself with basic exercises and master proper form.

Days per Week: 3 (e.g., Monday, Wednesday, Friday)

Routine

1. Squats (Bodyweight): 3 sets of 10 reps
2. Push-Ups (Knee or Wall Push-Ups if needed): 3 sets of 8 reps
3. Bent Over Dumbbell Rows: 3 sets of 10 reps
4. 3 sets of 8 repetitions for the dumbbell shoulder press
5. Plank: 3 sets, holding for 20-30 seconds

Weeks 3-4: Introduction to Resistance

Goal: Start incorporating weights, focusing on progressive overload.

Days per Week: 3

Routine

1. Goblet Squats (using a dumbbell): 3 sets of 10 reps
2. Push-Ups: 3 sets of 10 reps
3. Bent Over Dumbbell Rows: 3 sets of 12 reps
4. 3 sets of 10 repetitions for the dumbbell shoulder press
5. Plank: 3 sets, holding for 30-40 seconds

Weeks 5-6: Increasing Volume and Intensity

Goal: Challenge yourself by adding more volume and slightly more weight.

Days per Week: 4 (e.g., Monday, Tuesday, Thursday, Friday)

Routine

- Day 1 & 3 (Lower Body)

1. Goblet Squats: 4 sets of 12 reps
2. Lunges: 3 sets of 10 reps per leg
3. Glutei Bridges: 4 sets of 12 reps
4. Plank: 3 sets, holding for 45 seconds

- Day 2 & 4 (Upper Body)

1. Push-Ups: 4 sets of 12 reps
2. Bent Over Dumbbell Rows: 4 sets of 12 reps
3. Dumbbell Shoulder Press: 4 sets of 10 reps
4. Dumbbell Bicep Curls: 3 sets of 10 reps

5. Dumbbell Triceps Extensions: 3 sets of 10 reps

Weeks 7-8: Full Body Routines

Goal: Engage all major muscle groups in each session, with a focus on compound movements.

Days per Week: 3

Routine

1. Goblet Squats: 4 sets of 12 reps
2. Push-Ups: 4 sets of 12 reps
3. Lunges: 3 sets of 10 reps per leg
4. Bent Over Dumbbell Rows: 4 sets of 12 reps
5. 3 sets of 10 repetitions for the dumbbell shoulder press
6. Plank: 3 sets, holding for 50 seconds
7. Dumbbell Bicep Curls: 3 sets of 10 reps
8. Dumbbell Triceps Extensions: 3 sets of 10 reps

Guidelines & Tips

1. Warm-Up: Before every meeting, take part in a 5-10 moment warm-up. This can incorporate light cardio, dynamic stretches, or bodyweight workouts.

2. Rest: Permit 60-90 seconds of rest between sets. Rest days are similarly critical, giving your muscles time to recuperate and develop.

3. Moderate Overburden: Intend to slowly expand the weight you're lifting as the weeks go by. Be that as it may, consistently focus on the structure that is overweight.

4. Remain Hydrated: Hydrate all through your exercise to remain hydrated and help muscle capability.

5. Pay attention to Your Body: In the event that an activity feels excessively simple or excessively testing, change appropriately. Keep in mind it's tied in with building a solid groundwork and consistency.

Setting out on this 8-week venture is a promise to yourself and your well-being. By zeroing in on dominating structure and bit by bit testing yourself, you're establishing a hearty starting point for a future loaded with strength and imperativeness. Each rep, set, and drop of sweat is a demonstration of your devotion. Embrace the cycle, and praise the little.

Triumphs, and recall that as time passes, you're turning into a more grounded, more engaged form of yourself.

CHAPTER 8

NUTRITIONAL STRATEGIES FOR MUSCLE GROWTH AND FAT LOSS

It's frequently said, "You can't out-prepare a terrible eating routine," and this saying holds significant truth. While the thrill of lifting loads, starting to sweat, and pushing actual limits is unquestionable, genuine wizardry frequently mixes off the exercise center floor in our kitchens and eating tables. Sustenance is the overlooked yet truly great individual of any extraordinary wellness venture, the mind-boggling embroidered artwork winding around together muscle development, healing, and fat misfortune. Yet, with the staggering abundance of diets, enhancements, and guidance accessible, how can one explore this perplexing domain? In this section, we'll demystify the connection between food and fitness, offering noteworthy systems to fuel your body ideally. Whether you're expecting to shape fit muscle, shed undesirable pounds, or figures out some harmony between the two, understanding the cooperative energy of sustenance and training is the brilliant key. We should set out on this delightful excursion, where each chomp turns a bit nearer to your fitness objectives.

Macronutrient breakdown for strength training

Imagine carbohydrates as the gasoline for your car. They give the energy your body needs to ride out those overwhelming strength training sessions. At the point when you lift loads, your muscles use glycogen, which puts away glucose, as their essential wellspring of fuel. After an exercise, carbs assist with topping off those glycogen stores, guaranteeing you're trained for your next instructional course.

There are two primary sorts of carbs to know about:

Straightforward Carbs: Consider these as quick-consuming fuel. They're found in food varieties like products of the soil snacks. They can be helpful post-exercise when your body needs a speedy jolt of energy.

Complex Carbs: These are the gradually moving energy sources tracked down in entire grains, vegetables, and vegetables. They give a consistent inventory of energy and are extraordinary choices for your pre-exercise dinners.

For those who took part in strength training, carbs ought to make up a critical piece of your everyday calorie consumption, ordinarily around 45-65%.

Proteins: The Structure Blocks of Muscles

Proteins are the modelers and developers of your muscles. At the point when you lift loads, you make small tears in your muscle filaments. Proteins are responsible for fixing and modifying these filaments, making your muscles more grounded and bigger.

You can find proteins in different sources, like lean meats, fish, eggs, dairy items, vegetables, tofu, and temper. The suggested protein consumption for strength coaches goes from 1.2 to 2.2 grams per kilogram of body weight day to day, contingent upon your exercise power and recurrence.

Fats: The Uncelebrated yet Truly Great Individuals

Fats assume different parts in your solidarity preparing venture. They give a supported wellspring of energy during low-force exercises, guaranteeing you have the perseverance to finish your activities. Also, fats are fundamental for the development of chemicals like testosterone, which is vital for muscle development.

There are various kinds of fats to consider:

- **Soaked Fats:** Found in creature items and some plant oils, consuming these in moderation is ideal.

- **Unsaturated Fats:** Frequently alluded to as "great" fats, you can track down them in avocados, nuts, seeds, and olive oil. These fats support, generally speaking, well-being and prosperity.

- **Trans Fats:** These are typically tracked down in handled food sources and ought to stay away from them as they can have antagonistic well-being impacts.

Adjusting these macronutrients in your eating routine resembles coordinating an ensemble. Carbs give the prompt energy to begin the music, proteins construct the perplexing tunes of muscle, and fats guarantee the supported cadence of your solidarity-preparing venture. Keep in mind it's really not necessary to focus on barring any of these macronutrients but instead on orchestrating them to make the ideal tune for your wellness objectives.

Importance of hydration

Water, the remedy of life, moves through our reality like an uncelebrated yet genuinely great individual. It's not difficult to underestimate it, yet its nonattendance for even a brief time can set off a fountain of outcomes. Hydration, or the condition of keeping an ideal equilibrium of water in the body, is a fundamental part of general well-being. In this investigation, we should plunge into the significant significance of remaining very much hydrated, particularly with regard to regular daily existence and different proactive tasks, including strength training and workouts.

Prior to digging into the meaning of hydration, we should get a handle on the sheer degree of water's presence inside us. Our bodies are around 60% water, with this rate fluctuating based on age, orientation, and, generally speaking, well-being. However, it's not only a latent member; water is effectively engaged with basically every physical process.

Water plays a significant part in temperature guidelines. Our bodies keep an ideal temperature reach, and water helps in this guideline. It assimilates and delivers heat gradually, permitting us to adapt to natural temperature vacillations.

In the domain of processing and supplement retention, legitimate processing and retention of supplements happen in a water-based climate. Water helps separate food, making it more straightforward for the body to remove fundamental accessories.

Water is additionally the soul of our transportation framework. Blood, the body's transportation organization, is fundamentally made out of water. It conveys oxygen, supplements, and chemicals to different cells and eliminates side effects for discharge.

With regard to joint well-being, water plays a pivotal part in oil. The synovial liquid that pads and greases up our joints is water-based. Remaining hydrated is crucial for keeping up with joint well-being and adaptability.

Also, water upholds the end of byproducts through pee, sweat, and defecation. Sufficient hydration is essential for the body's normal detoxification processes.

Now that we comprehend the crucial job of water, how about we investigate the results of parchedness:

Indeed, even a gentle lack of hydration can prompt diminished energy levels and weariness. Your body needs to work harder to perform routine undertakings, leaving you feeling tired.

Drying out can debilitate mental capabilities like fixation, sharpness, and momentary memory. It could influence temperament, possibly prompting expanded sensations of stress and tension.

During exercise, particularly strength training, a lack of hydration can prompt diminished perseverance, strength, and, by and large, athletic execution. It expands the gamble of muscle issues and intensity-related sicknesses.

Drying out can likewise prompt stomach-related issues, as the body battles to handle food and take out squander.

In sweltering climates or during actual severe work, the gamble of intensity-related diseases like intensity fatigue or heatstroke essentially expands when you're dried out.

Strength training, which frequently includes thorough effort and sweat, puts explicit expectations on your body's hydration levels. Appropriate hydration is critical in light of multiple factors:

Lack of hydration can hinder muscle capability, prompting diminished strength and perseverance during exercises. This hampers your presentation as well as limits your possible increases.

Legitimate hydration can assist with forestalling muscle squeezes, a typical event during strength training. Got dried-out muscles are more inclined to fit and squeeze.

Post-exercise, hydration helps with the recuperation interaction. It helps transport supplements to muscle cells, working with fix and development.

Strength training can raise your internal heat level. Satisfactory hydration helps with managing your inner temperature, diminishing the gamble of overheating.

Commonsense hydration tips incorporate observing the shade of your pee, drinking previously, during, and after working out, paying attention to your body's thirst signals, taking into account electrolyte-rich refreshments for extraordinary exercises, and keeping a decent eating routine wealthy in products of the soil, which generally contain water and add to in general hydration.

All things being equal, hydration isn't just about tasting water; it's tied in with respecting your body's requirement for balance. In the domain of solidarity preparing and day-to-day existence the same, the meaning of remaining satisfactorily hydrated couldn't possibly be more significant. The help supports your body's capabilities and guarantees you perform at your best, whether you're lifting loads or just making every second count.

Supplements: Which are beneficial?

Chasing ideal well-being and wellness, numerous people go to enhancements to connect expected dietary holes, upgrade execution, or support explicit objectives. While a decent eating regimen ought to provide a large portion of the supplements our bodies need, there are circumstances where enhancements can be valuable. In this investigation, we'll dig into a few commonly utilized enhancements and when they may be profitable, with an emphasis on how they connect with strength training and workouts.

1. Protein Enhancements

What They Are: Protein supplements, like whey, casein, and plant-based protein powders, are concentrated wellsprings of protein obtained from different sources.

At the point when they're gainful: Protein enhancements can be helpful for people who battle to meet their every day protein necessities through food alone. This can be particularly important for strength mentors expecting to fabricate and fix muscle tissue.

How They Help: Protein supplements give an advantageous and speedy method for expanding protein consumption, especially after exercises when protein union is uplifted. They can support muscle recovery and development when consumed in conjunction with strength training.

2. Creatine

Creatine is a commonly occurring compound tracked down in limited quantities in specific food sources and delivered by the body. Creatine supplements regularly come as Creatine monohydrates.

At the point when it's beneficial: Creatine is notable for its presentation-improved impacts, especially in exercises that require short eruptions of extreme exertion, like weightlifting and running.

How It Makes a Difference: Creatine supplementation can expand the body's creatine phosphate stores, which are utilized as a quick wellspring of energy during extreme-focus, short-term exercises. This can prompt superior strength, power, and muscle perseverance.

3. Fanned Chain Amino Acids (BCAAs)

BCAAs are a gathering of fundamental amino acids: leucine, isoleucine, and valine.

At the point when They're helpful: BCAAs are commonly utilized as enhancements to help muscle recuperation and decrease muscle irritation, which can be especially valuable for those who participate in extraordinary strength training.

How They Help: BCAAs are accepted to lessen muscle protein breakdown during exercise and advance protein blend. This can prompt diminished muscle harm and speedier recovery between workouts.

4. Fish Oil (Omega-3 Unsaturated fats)

Fish oil supplements contain omega-3 unsaturated fats, explicitly eicosapentaenoic corrosive (EPA) and docosahexaenoic corrosive (DHA).

At the point when It's valuable: Omega-3 enhancements can be helpful for their calming properties, which might support diminishing activity-induced irritation and advancing joint well-being.

How It Makes a Difference: Omega-3 unsaturated fats are known for their calming impacts, which can assist with relieving the irritation and muscle touchiness that occasionally follow extreme exercises. They may likewise uphold cardiovascular well-being.

5. Vitamin D

Vitamin D is a fat-solvent nutrient that assumes a critical role in calcium retention and bone well-being.

At the point when it's Valuable, Vitamin D supplementation might be necessary for people who have restricted sun openness or those with a lack, which is moderately normal in specific locales.

How It Makes a Difference: Vitamin D is fundamental for keeping up with bone well-being and muscle capability. Deficient levels can prompt debilitated bones and decreased muscle strength, the two of which can influence strength training execution.

6. Caffeine

Caffeine is a characteristic energizer tracked down in espresso, tea, and different enhancements.

At the point when it's valuable: Caffeine supplements are frequently utilized as execution enhancers because of their animating impacts on the focal sensory system.

How It Makes a Difference: Caffeine can increment readiness, diminish apparent exertion during activity, and improve perseverance and strength, making it a well-known decision for competitors and strength mentors.

7. Beta-Alanine

Beta-alanine is a usually happening amino corrosive that is utilized to deliver carnosine, a compound that helps cradle lactic corrosive in muscles.

At the point when It's Gainful: Beta-alanine supplements are frequently used to develop perseverance during extreme focus exercises further, making them significant for strength coaches.

How It Makes a Difference: By expanding muscle carnosine levels, beta-alanine can postpone the beginning of muscle exhaustion and decrease muscle corrosiveness, permitting people to push through testing exercises with less distress.

8. Iron

Iron is a fundamental mineral expected for the development of hemoglobin, which transports oxygen in the blood.

At the point when it's Gainful: Iron supplementation might be necessary for people with iron-inadequacy sickliness, which can prompt weakness and diminished practice execution.

How It Makes a Difference: Iron supplementation can address weakness, increment red platelet creation, and further develop oxygen conveyance to muscles, possibly upgrading perseverance and, generally speaking, strength training limit.

9. Multivitamins

Multivitamins are supplements that contain a mix of nutrients and minerals.

At the point when they're Gainful: Multivitamins can be helpful for people with explicit dietary limitations or lacks, guaranteeing they meet their day-to-day supplement needs.

How They Help: By giving a wide range of fundamental nutrients and minerals, multivitamins assist with filling possible nourishing holes and backing, generally speaking, well-being, which can, in a roundabout way, influence strength training progress.

10. Pre-Exercise Enhancements

Pre-exercise supplements regularly contain a mix of fixings like caffeine, amino acids, and nitric oxide promoters.

At the point when they're helpful: Pre-exercise supplements are intended to upgrade energy, concentration, and exercise execution. They can be utilized when an additional lift is wanted.

How They Help: Pre-exercise enhancements can work on mental sharpness, increment inspiration, and give the energy expected to serious strength instructional meetings.

While these enhancements can offer advantages, it's crucial to approach supplementation insightfully. Counsel with a medical care supplier or enrolled dietitian can assist with deciding individual requirements, likely lacks, and the most suitable enhancements for explicit objectives. Moreover, enhancements ought to supplement a fair eating routine and not supplant entire food sources as the essential wellspring of supplements. In the domain of strength training and working out, enhancements can act as significant devices. However, they should be coordinated into a far-reaching approach that focuses on nourishment, hydration, and general well-being.

CHAPTER 9

ADVANCED TECHNIQUES AND PLATEAU BREAKING

As you venture through the domain of strength training, you'll definitely experience levels—those disappointing minutes when your advancement appears to slow down. These levels can be frustrating, but on the other hand, they're valuable and open doors for development and progression. In this section, we'll investigate progressed procedures that can assist you with getting through these obstructions, revive your strength training schedule, and proceed with your way toward accomplishing your wellness objectives.

Strength training is an assertive discipline, and what worked for you as a fledgling might yield various outcomes when you become more experienced. Levels are a characteristic piece of this development, flagging that your body has adjusted to your ongoing everyday practice. Nonetheless, by consolidating progressed procedures and systems, you can reignite your advancement, challenge your muscles in new ways, and drive your limits farther than at any other time.

All through this section, we'll dive into different high-level training strategies, like periodization, high-level activity varieties, and specific training conventions. You'll find how these procedures can assist you with upgrading your strength training routine, staying away from stagnation, and accomplishing new degrees of execution and strong turns of events. Thus, gear up and prepare to investigate the intriguing universe of cutting-edge strength training techniques, where the excursion of progress never genuinely arrives at its last objective.

Incorporating techniques like drop sets, supersets, and paused reps

As you progress in your strength training venture, the requirement for assortment and difficulties becomes progressively apparent. What worked in the beginning phases may yield different outcomes as your body adjusts and levels. This is where best-in-class training methods like drop sets, supersets, and stopped reps become the most critical factors. These strategies present new difficulties, heighten your exercises, and animate muscle development in unique ways. In this investigation, we'll dive into every one of these methods, making sense of how and when to integrate them into your strength training schedule.

1. Drop Sets: Releasing the Force of Weariness

What Are Drop Sets: Drop sets, otherwise called strip sets or sliding sets, include playing out a progression of back-to-back sets for a similar activity with negligible in the middle between. Notwithstanding, there's a bend—you logically diminish the load after each set while going for the gold.

When to Utilize Drop Sets: Drop sets are compelling when you need to push your muscles as far as possible and increment metabolic pressure, which can contribute to muscle development. They're accommodating for getting through strength levels and building perseverance.

Step-by-step instructions to integrate drop sets:

- Pick an activity and decide your beginning weight, generally around 70-80% of your one-rep max (1RM).
- Play out a bunch of 8-12 reps with this weight, arriving at close to solid disappointment.
- Promptly diminish the load by 20-30% and play out one more set to disappointment.
- Rehash this interaction for 2-3 drop sets, step by step, diminishing the weight each time.

2. Supersets: Expanding Proficiency and Force

What Are Supersets: Supersets include matching two distinct activities and performing them successively with negligible to no in the middle between. There are two principal sorts of supersets: adversarial and agonistic.

- Hostile Supersets: This type includes working contradicting muscle bunches in a solitary set. For instance, matching bicep twists with rear arm muscle augmentations.
- Agonistic Supersets: Here, you focus on a similar muscle bunch with two unique activities. For example, consolidating seat presses with push-ups.

When to Utilize Supersets: Supersets are perfect for time-effective exercises and expanding training thickness. They can assist you with boosting muscle enlistment, upgrading perseverance, and working on solid definition.

Instructions to Integrate Supersets:

- Select two activities that complete one another as far as muscle gatherings or development designs.
- Perform one bunch of the principal workout, quickly followed by one bunch of the subsequent activity.
- Rest for a short period (usually 30 seconds to 1 moment) and rehash for the ideal number of sets.

3. Stopped Reps: Developing Fortitude and Control

What Are Stopped Reps: Stopped reps include momentarily stopping at a particular point during a reiteration, commonly at the midpoint of the most challenging period of activity.

When to Utilize Stopped Reps: Stopped reps are excellent for further developing strength, method, and muscle commitment. They're instrumental when you need to conquer staying focused in a lift or upgrade muscle enactment.

Step-by-step instructions to Integrate Stopped Reps:

- Pick an activity and decide the fitting point in the scope of movement for the respite.
- Play out a reiteration of the activity and respite at the assigned point for 1-3 seconds.
- Proceed with the redundancy to the end, zeroing in on control and legitimate structure.
- Rehash for the ideal number of reps and sets.

Rules for Securely Integrating Progressed Procedures:

1. **Progress Slowly**: In the event that you're new to these methods, begin with lower power and steadily increment the test. This diminishes the gamble of injury.

2.   **Maintain Appropriate Structure:** No matter what the method, focus on legitimate structure and strategy to guarantee security and viability.

3.   **Listen to Your Body**: Give close consideration to how your body answers these procedures. Change the power and volume on a case-by-case basis to keep away from overtraining or unreasonable weakness.

4.   **Plan Recuperation:** Bring progressed methods decisively into your training program and consider sufficient recuperation between serious meetings.

5.   **Combine Methods:** You can consolidate drop sets, supersets, and stopped reps in your exercises to make an assortment and challenge your muscles from different points.

6.   **Consult an Expert:** On the off chance that you're uncertain about how to integrate these procedures into your everyday practice or have any worries, consider counseling a confirmed fitness mentor or mentor.

Consolidating progressed preparing procedures like drop sets, supersets, and stopped reps can reinvigorate your strength training routine. These strategies get through levels as well as change up your exercises. Recall that the way to fruitful execution is an insightful methodology that lines up with your objectives and focuses on security and recovery. Whether you're going for the gold hypertrophy, further developed perseverance, or improved strength, these procedures can be essential instruments in your fitness process.

How to recognize and overcome training plateaus

Training levels resemble thorny barricades on your wellness process. Eventually, progress appears to slow down, leaving you disappointed and thinking about what turned out badly. Fortunately, levels are an ordinary piece of any strength training project, and they can be overwhelmed with the correct methodology. In this conversation, we'll investigate how to perceive when you've hit a level and give pragmatic procedures to get through it.

Perceiving a Level

Levels are times of stagnation, where your exhibition or muscle development seems to stop regardless of predictable exertion. Here are a few signs that you may be amidst a level:

1. **Lack of Progress:** You last saw enhancements in your strength, perseverance, or muscle definition quite a long time ago or even months ago.

2. **Decreased Inspiration:** You're feeling less persuaded or excited about your exercises since you need to see the outcomes you anticipate.

3.   Consistent Daily practice: You've been following a similar exercise routine daily practice and involving similar loads and redundancies for a drawn-out period.

4.   Fatigue and Disappointment: You might be encountering weakness, both honestly and intellectually, and dissatisfaction is sneaking in.

Procedures to Beat Levels

Getting through a level requires a mix of persistence, methodology, and flexibility. This is the way to handle it:

1.   Change Your Daily schedule: Levels frequently happen on the grounds that your body has adjusted to your ongoing everyday practice. Change everything around by modifying your activities, the request for your exercises, or the power of your meetings.

2.   Progressive Overburden: Continuously increment the weight you lift or the power of your activities. This ever-evolving over-burden difficulties your muscles and animates development.

3.   Vary Redundancy Reaches: Tests with various reiteration ranges, like lower reps with heavier loads or higher reps with lighter loads. This variety can stun your muscles into development.

4.   **Focus on Flimsy spots:** Recognize your shortcomings and commit additional regard for those areas. This designated approach can assist you with getting through levels in unambiguous lifts or muscle gatherings.

5.   **Nutritional Appraisal:** Audit your eating routine to guarantee you're getting the proper equilibrium of macronutrients and calories. Sufficient nourishment is vital for muscle development and recovery.

6.   **Recovery and Rest:** Guarantee you're getting sufficient rest and quality rest. Recovery is the point at which your body fixes and develops further.

7.   **Reduce Pressure:** High feelings of anxiety can impede progress. Execute pressure-decrease methods like contemplation, yoga, or care rehearses.

8.   **Track Your Advancement:** Keep a definite training diary to screen your exercises, including sets, reps, and loads utilized. This can assist you with recognizing examples and making essential changes.

9.   **Consider Deloading:** Once in a while, a deload week where you lessen the power and volume of your exercises can help your body recuperate and get through a level.

10.   **Consult a Mentor or Mentor:** On the off chance that you've attempted different techniques and can't beat a level,

consider looking for direction from a certified fitness mentor or coach. They can give customized guidance and make another arrangement custom-made to your objectives.

11.   Stay Steady: Levels can be deterred. However, consistency is vital. Continue to appear for your exercises in any event when progress seems to be slow. Recall that levels are transitory.

12.   Set Reasonable Objectives: Guarantee your objectives are attainable and sensible. Here and there, ridiculous assumptions can prompt disappointment during levels.

Getting through a training level can be testing, but on the other hand, it's a chance for development and improvement. Remember that levels are a characteristic piece of the fitness venture, and with the right outlook and procedures, you can defeat them. Remain versatile, remain roused, and recollect that progress is a cycle that frequently includes highs and lows.

CHAPTER 10

STRENGTH TRAINING DURING PREGNANCY AND POSTPARTUM

Pregnancy and the post-pregnancy time frame are groundbreaking stages in a woman's life, both genuinely and inwardly. They bring an interesting arrangement of difficulties and potential open doors, including contemplations for keeping up with or in any event, beginning a strength training schedule. In this section, we will dig into the complexities of strength training during pregnancy and post pregnancy, giving direction, security tips, and exercise proposals to assist you with exploring this surprising excursion with certainty and care. Whether you're an accomplished strength coach or new to the universe of wellness, this section will offer important bits of knowledge into how to focus on your wellbeing and prosperity during this groundbreaking time.

Safe exercise recommendations during each trimester

Here is a more story-style guide for safe activity during every trimester of pregnancy:

First Trimester (Week 1 to Week 12)

The primary trimester is a period of change. Your body is adjusting to pregnancy, and moving toward practice with care is critical. Start by counseling your medical care supplier to guarantee that exercise is all right for your unique circumstances.

In the primary trimester, you might encounter weariness and morning affliction. It's fundamental to pay attention to your body. On the off chance that you feel tired, relax. Assuming that you experience nausea, consider gentler types of activity like strolling or pre-birth yoga.

Second Trimester (Week 13 to Week 27)

Numerous women view the second trimester as the most agreeable for working out. Queasiness frequently dies down, and energy levels move along. Average registrations with your medical care supplier are fundamental.

Moderate-power cardio, like energetic strolling or swimming, can assist you with keeping up with cardiovascular fitness without overexertion. Strength training with light to direct loads is likewise gainful; however, try not to do weighty lifts and activities that strain your mid-region.

Third Trimester (Week 28 to Week 40+)

As you enter the third trimester, your body goes through massive changes to oblige your developing child. Exercise can assist with setting you up for labor and lift your general prosperity.

Consider pre-birth yoga to upgrade adaptability and unwinding methods. Water heart-stimulating exercise is an astounding decision for easing the tension in your joints. Strolling stays a low-influence choice for cardiovascular activity.

It's fundamental to discuss consistently with your medical care supplier and change your daily workout practice on a case-by-case basis. As you progress, you might have to lessen the force and length of your exercises—center around remaining agreeable, hydrated, and very much refreshed.

All through your pregnancy, focus on your security and the prosperity of your child. By observing these trimester-explicit activity rules, you can remain dynamic and get ready for the unimaginable excursion of labor and post-pregnancy recuperation.

Regaining strength and muscle post-pregnancy

Pregnancy is a delightful and groundbreaking experience, yet it likewise puts attractive expectations on your body. As another mother, recovering strength and muscle post-pregnancy is an objective that can assist you with exploring the actual difficulties of parenthood and lift your general prosperity.

Grasping Post pregnancy Changes

Pregnancy and labor achieve tremendous changes in your body. During pregnancy, your muscles and joints adjust to oblige your developing child, and hormonal vacillations assume an urgent part in these changes. Subsequent to conceiving an offspring, your body goes through a progressive recuperation process.

One typical concern post-pregnancy is the partition of stomach muscles, known as diastasis recti. It's fundamental to recognize these progressions and move toward your post-pregnancy fitness venture with care and persistence.

Focusing on Security and Interview

Prior to leaving any post-pregnancy practice program, counseling your medical care provider is essential. They can survey your singular well-being and give customized suggestions in view of your remarkable conditions.

Early Post pregnancy Weeks (0-6)

During the quick post-pregnancy time frame, rest and recovery are central. These weeks are tied in withholding with your child and permitting your body to recuperate. Delicate developments, for example, profound breathing and pelvic floor workouts, can advance the flow and backing of the recuperating system.

Early Post pregnancy Stage (6-12 Weeks)

Around a month and a half post-pregnancy, you can, step by step, once again introduce actual work. Begin with short strolls, which serve not exclusively to advance cardiovascular well-being but also to reduce post-pregnancy uneasiness. Bodyweight practices like squats rushes, and altered push-ups are fantastic decisions to start modifying muscle tone.

Mid-Post pregnancy Stage (12-24 Weeks)

As you progress into the mid-post-pregnancy stage, you can consolidate obstruction groups for delicate opposition in activities, for example, bicep twists, lines, and leg lifts. Center reinforcing works out, particularly assuming that you had diastasis recti, ought to be performed under proficient direction. Light free weights can likewise be presented for situated shoulder squeezes, chest presses, and leg augmentations.

Late Post pregnancy and then some (24+ Weeks)

In the late post-pregnancy stage and then some, you can grow your strength by training the schedule. Consolidate a balanced program that objectives significant muscle gatherings, including compound activities like squats, deadlifts, and seat presses. Progressively increment the loads and protection to challenge your muscles and advance development. Cardiovascular exercises like running, swimming, or cycling can likewise be incorporated to help perseverance and, in general, wellness.

Extra Contemplations

•   **Breastfeeding:** Assuming you're breastfeeding, be aware of your energy and supplement needs. Guarantee you polish off an adequate number of calories and remain hydrated to help both your wellness process and milk creation.

•   **Recuperation and Rest:** Focus on rest and recovery days to permit your body to mend and adjust to work out. Your body has experienced massive changes, and it needs time to recuperate.

•   **Standing by listening to Your Body**: Give close consideration to your body's signs during exercise. Assuming that you experience uneasiness or torment, counseling your medical care supplier for guidance is fundamental.

Each woman's post-pregnancy venture is novel, and it's urgent to adjust your daily workout practice to your particular requirements and solace level. The post-pregnancy time frame isn't just about recovering actual essentialness but also about taking care of oneself and strengthening. Praise your advancement en route, and recollect that as you remake your strength and muscle, you're additionally embracing the unimaginable changes and obligations that parenthood brings.

CHAPTER 11

STRENGTH TRAINING FOR MATURE WOMEN

Strength training is an immortal pursuit that offers unimaginable advantages at each phase of life. In this part, we shift our concentration to the unique universe of solidarity preparing for mature women. As we age, our bodies go through different changes, including muscle misfortune, bone thickness decrease, and changes in hormonal equilibrium. Strength training is an incredible asset to check these age-related changes, upgrade general prosperity, and advance dynamic and satisfying lives.

Whether you're a lover or simply starting your strength training venture sometime down the road, this section is custom-fitted to address the particular necessities, contemplations, and benefits of solidarity preparing for mature women. We'll investigate the various advantages, well-being rules, and exercise suggestions to assist you with remaining solid, dynamic, and versatile as you embrace the magnificence of maturing with strength and certainty.

Addressing hormonal changes during menopause

Menopause is a characteristic stage in a woman's life, commonly happening in her late 40s or mid-50s when her periods stop. This critical organic progress achieves a vast number of changes, remembering variances in hormonal levels. While menopause is an ordinary piece of maturing, it can likewise introduce exceptional difficulties, both honestly and inwardly.

One of the vital hormonal changes that women experience during menopause is a critical decline in estrogen creation. This hormonal shift can differently affect the body, remembering a diminishing bone thickness, an expanded gamble of coronary illness, and changes in body piece, frequently prompting weight gain and a rearrangement of fat.

While these progressions are a characteristic piece of the maturing system, it's critical to recognize that they can likewise be tended to and overseen. This is where strength training steps in as a vital partner.

Figuring out the Job of Chemicals in Menopause

Estrogen, progesterone, and testosterone are essential chemicals that play a massive part in a woman's well-being and prosperity all through her life. During menopause, estrogen creation declines fundamentally. This hormonal shift can make far-reaching impacts:

1.   **Bone Well-being:** Estrogen assumes an imperative part in keeping up with bone thickness. Decreased estrogen levels can prompt a higher gamble of osteoporosis and cracks.

2.   **Heart Well-being**: Estrogen likewise defensively affects the cardiovascular framework. A decrease in estrogen can expand the gamble of coronary illness.

3.   **Muscle and Digestion**: Lower estrogen levels can add to muscle misfortune and changes in digestion, which can prompt weight gain and changes in body structure.

4.   **Mood and Rest:** Hormonal vacillations during menopause can influence the state of mind, rest examples, and, by an enormous, profound prosperity.

Strength Training as an Answer

Strength training, frequently alluded to as obstruction or power lifting, is a profoundly viable method for balancing the physical and metabolic changes that go with menopause. This is the way strength training can address these difficulties:

1.   **Bone Well-being:** Weight-bearing activities, for example, lifting loads or performing obstruction works out, animate bone arrangement and help keep up with or increment bone thickness. This is pivotal for diminishing the gamble of osteoporosis and breaks.

2. Muscle Conservation: Strength training assists in protecting and working with muscling mass, which can check the average decrease in muscle that happens with age. Keeping up with bulk is fundamental for digestion, as power consumes a more significant number of calories, very still than fat.

3. Metabolism: As bulk expands or is protected through strength training, your digestion gets a lift. This can assist with forestalling weight gain and changes in body creation usually connected with menopause.

4. Heart Well-being: Strength training can definitely affect heart well-being by further developing pulse, diminishing irritation, and advancing general cardiovascular wellness.

5. Mood and Rest: Exercise, including strength training, has been displayed to decrease side effects of uneasiness and sorrow, further develop rest quality, and improve the general state of mind and prosperity.

Start with Strength training

On the off chance that you're new to strength preparing or have restricted insight, it's crucial to start gradually and look for direction:

1. Consult an Expert: Prior to starting any activity program, particularly on the off chance that you have hidden ailments, talk with a confirmed wellness mentor or medical care supplier to guarantee that strength training is protected and fit for you.

2. **Learn Appropriate Structure:** It's significant to get familiar with the proper structure and strategy for strength training works. Legitimate design lessens the gamble of injury and amplifies the advantages of every development.

3. **Gradual Movement:** Begin with light loads or obstruction groups and continuously increment the force as you become more agreeable and certain.

4. **Variety:** Integrate various activities that target different muscle gatherings. This guarantees a fair and complete gym routine every practice.

5. **Consistency:** Consistency is vital to seeing long-haul benefits. Go for the gold instructional courses in a perfect world a few times each week.

6. **Nutrition and Hydration:** Keep a decent eating regimen and remain very hydrated to help your fitness objectives and general well-being.

Embracing the force of strength training

Menopause is a groundbreaking stage in a woman's life, and keeping in mind that it accompanies its one-of-a-kind arrangement of difficulties, it likewise presents open doors for development and prosperity. Strength training is a significant device that can assist you with exploring this excursion with strength, flexibility, and certainty.

By tending to hormonal changes through standard strength training, you can advance bone well-being, keep up with bulk, support your digestion, and work on, generally speaking, cardiovascular wellness. Besides, the advantages stretch out past the physical; the practice has been displayed to decidedly affect the state of mind, close-to-home prosperity, and rest quality, all of which can improve your general personal satisfaction during menopause and then some.

Strength training isn't just about lifting loads; it's tied in with embracing the force of your body to adjust, develop, and flourish. As you set out on this excursion, recall that you can shape your well-being and prosperity all through menopause and into your later years.

Bone health and osteoporosis prevention

At the point when we ponder well-being and fitness, it's easy to zero in on muscles, cardiovascular well-being, and general prosperity. Notwithstanding, the strength and soundness of our bones are similarly fundamental but frequently ignored parts of our actual imperativeness. Keeping up severe strength areas isn't just essential for ordinary exercises but also helps forestall a condition that influences a great many individuals around the world: osteoporosis.

Grasping Osteoporosis

Osteoporosis is a condition characterized by debilitated and weak bones, making them more vulnerable to cracks and breaks. It frequently advances quietly, with practically no side effects, until a suspension happens. Everyday locales for vacations because of osteoporosis incorporate the hip, spine, and wrist. While osteoporosis can influence all kinds of people, it is more typical in women, especially as they age and move toward menopause.

The Job of Bone Thickness

Bone thickness is a proportion of the strength and thickness of your bones. It's affected by different variables, including hereditary qualities, way of life, and hormonal changes. Top bone thickness is commonly reached in early adulthood, and afterward, it slowly declines with age.

Hormonal Changes and Bone Well-being

Hormonal changes assume a critical role in bone well-being, especially in women. Estrogen, a chemical that diminishes essentially during menopause, plays a pivotal role in keeping up with bone thickness. The decrease in estrogen levels can speed up bone misfortune, prompting osteoporosis now and again.

Forestalling Osteoporosis through Way of Life Decisions

While certain variables influencing bone thickness are unchangeable as far as we might be concerned, there is a way we can make life decisions to advance bone well-being and decrease the risk of osteoporosis:

1.   **Dietary Calcium**: Calcium is an indispensable mineral for bone well-being. Guarantee you devour a satisfactory measure of calcium-rich food sources like dairy items, salad greens, and invigorated food sources, or think about supplements if essential.

2.   **Vitamin D:** Vitamin D is fundamental for calcium assimilation. Investing energy in the sun and eating food varieties plentiful in vitamin D, like greasy fish and sustained grains, can help.

3.   **Regular Activity:** Weight-bearing activities like strolling, running, and strength training advance bone thickness. Strength training, specifically, helps fabricate and keep up with muscle, which can offer help to your bones.

4.   **Quit Smoking:** Smoking is related to lower bone thickness. Stopping smoking can help your general well-being, including your bones.

5.   Limit Liquor: Unreasonable liquor utilization can debilitate bones. Restricting liquor admission can add to bone well-being.

6.   Bone Thickness Testing: Consider bone thickness testing, particularly on the off chance that you have risk factors for osteoporosis. Early discovery takes into account proactive measures.

The Job of Solidarity Preparing

Strength training is a champion in the domain of osteoporosis counteraction. This is the way it adds to bone well-being:

1.   Bone Stacking: Strength training puts weight on bones, which invigorates the body to assemble more bone thickness to endure the additional heap. This assists with keeping up with and incrementing bone thickness.

2.   Muscle Help: Solid muscles offer help to your bones, diminishing the gamble of falls and breaks.

3.   Improved Equilibrium: Strength training practices that target equilibrium and security can improve coordination and lessen the probability of falls.

4.   Maintaining Freedom: Solid bones and muscles are fundamental for day-to-day exercises and keeping up with autonomy as you age.

Integrating strength training into your wellness standard, regardless of whether you're different from it, can be a strong move toward protecting your bone well-being. It's never past time to begin. Talk with a wellness expert to make a strength-preparing plan that suits your requirements and capacities.

Recollect that bone well-being is a deep-rooted venture. Your decisions today can fundamentally affect your bone thickness and, by and large, prosperity as you age. By focusing on your eating routine, participating in the standard activity, especially strength training, and embracing a bone-sound way of life, you can find proactive ways to forestall osteoporosis and appreciate solid, versatile bones all through your life.

Adjustments and considerations for older adults

Strength training is an exceptional type of activity that offers various medical advantages, paying little mind to maturity. Nonetheless, as we get older, our bodies go through changes that require explicit changes and contemplations while taking part in strength training. In this extensive aid, we will dig into the significance of strength training for more established adults, dig into the physiological changes that happen with maturing, and give helpful appeals and changes in accordance with a protected and successful strength training routine.

The Meaning of strength training for More established Grown-ups

Strength training, frequently known as obstruction or power lifting, involves using outer protection to challenge muscles and upgrade their strength. It gives a large number of benefits to more established adults, including:

1. Muscle Protection: Maturing is often joined by muscle misfortune, known as sarcopenia, which can prompt shortcomings and a decrease in practical capacities. Strength training assists with keeping up with or even improving bulk, bringing about better overall capability.

2. Bone Well-being: As we age, the risk of osteoporosis, described by delicate and fragile bones, increases. Weight-bearing activities, for example, strength training, invigorate bone turnover and thickness and lessen the probability of cracks.

3. Further developed digestion: muscles consume a more significant number of calories than fat, so expanding bulk can assist with maintaining a solid weight and metabolic rate.

4. Upgraded Practical Freedom: Strength training upgrades equilibrium, coordination, and dependability, bringing down the risk of falls and working on regular exercises and autonomy.

5. The board of Constant Illnesses: Strength training has been exhibited to assist with overseeing persistent circumstances like diabetes, joint pain, and coronary illness.

Physiological Changes with Maturing

To appreciate the changes and contemplations for more seasoned adults in strength training, it's urgent to get a handle on the physiological changes that go with the maturing system:

1. Bulk Misfortune: Sarcopenia, the age-related decrease in bulk, can start as soon as one's 30s. After the age of 50, muscle misfortune can speed up, bringing about diminished strength and muscle capability.

2. Lessened Bone Thickness: With maturation, bone thickness typically diminishes, making bones more vulnerable to cracks.

3. More slow digestion: Maturing frequently achieves a drop in metabolic rate, making it more straightforward to put on weight and more complicated to safeguard muscle.

4. Joint Alterations: Joints are not so much adaptable but rather more inclined to firmness, expanding the risk of conditions like osteoarthritis.

5. Equilibrium and Coordination: Diminishes in equilibrium and coordination elevate the gamble of falls.

Changes and Contemplations for More Established Grown-ups

1. Clinical Freedom: Prior to leaving on a strength training routine, especially in the event that you have previous ailments or are taking meds, counsel your medical care supplier for clinical leeway and customized suggestions for your well-being status.

2. Slow Commencement: In the event that you are new to strength training or returning after a lengthy break, start continuously. Begin with light loads or opposition groups to permit your muscles and joints to adjust constantly.

3. Underscore Legitimate Structure: The proper structure is essential to forestall injury. Think about working with a guaranteed wellness mentor to become familiar with the reasonable procedures for different activities.

4. Consolidate Warm-Up and Chill-Off: Remember warm-up and chill-off practices for your daily schedule to set up your body for practice and advance adaptability and portability.

5. Embrace Moderate Overburden: Step by step, increment the opposition or weight in your strength training schedule. This movement challenges your muscles and advances their development.

6. Keep up with Scope of Movement: Focus on keeping up with and working on your scope of movement. Adaptability, like extending, can assist with balancing strength.

7. Improve Equilibrium and Soundness: Incorporate equilibrium and dependability practices into your daily schedule to upgrade coordination and lessen the risk of falls.

8. Fortify Your Center: Center muscle reinforcing can further develop steadiness and back your spine, bringing down the risk of back torment.

9. Tune into Your Body: Be mindful of any inconvenience or agony during exercise. On the off chance that you experience torment, stop the activity and counsel a medical services supplier or fitness professional.

10. Hydration and Nourishment: Remain hydrated enough and keep a reasonable eating regimen to help muscle development and, generally speaking, well-being.

11. Focus on Rest and Recuperation: Satisfactory rest and recovery periods between strength instructional meetings are essential for muscle fix and development.

12. Consistency Is Vital: Ordinary-strength instructional courses, in a perfect world, 2-3 times each week, are critical to seeing improvement.

13. Flexibility: Be available to adjust your strength training routine depending on the situation to accommodate actual limits or changes in your well-being.

14. Encourage social commitment: Consider joining bunch strength instructional courses or finding an exercise accomplice to help inspire social communication.

Test Strength Training Project for More Seasoned Grown-ups

Here is an example of a strength training program that is reasonable for more seasoned adults. Remember that you ought to change the activities and loads in light of your singular capacities and fitness level:

Warm-up (5–10 minutes)

- Light cardiovascular activity (e.g., strolling or fixed cycling)
- Delicate dynamic stretches (e.g., leg swings and arm circles)

Strength Preparing (20-30 minutes)

- Squats: 2 arrangements of 10-12 reiterations
- Push-Ups (or changed push-ups against a wall or ledge): 2 arrangements of 8-10 reiterations

- Twisted around weight Lines (or opposition band columns): 2 arrangements of 10-12 reiterations
- Standing Free weight Shoulder Press (or situated press): 2 arrangements of 8-10 redundancies
- Leg Raises (to reinforce center muscles): 2 arrangements of 10-12 reiterations

Cool-Down (5-10 minutes)

- Static extending to upgrade adaptability and decrease muscle pressure
- Center around significant muscle gatherings, including legs, arms, chest, back, and shoulders

Equilibrium and dependability (5-10 minutes, depending on the situation)

- Remaining on one leg with eyes open and shut
- Heel-to-toe strolling
- Balance practices utilizing a security ball or equilibrium board

Strength training remains a powerful instrument for keeping up with and working on, by and large, well-being and capability as one ages. By appreciating the physiological changes that go with maturing and carrying out fundamental changes and contemplations, people can enjoy the large number of advantages presented by strength training excellent into their brilliant years. Whether you are a novice to strength training or a carefully prepared devotee, consistently recollect that a very organized and customized program can help you protect strength, portability, and essentialness all through your lifetime. For direction and clinical opportunity, it is essential to talk with your clinical consideration supplier prior to starting any action program, particularly assuming you suspect that you have undiscovered ailments or concerns.

CHAPTER 12

INJURY PREVENTION AND MANAGEMENT

In the excursion of strength training, the quest for fitness and prosperity frequently accompanies the gamble of wounds. Whether you're a carefully prepared competitor or simply starting your strength training experience, understanding injury counteraction and the board is essential to keeping a sound and manageable training schedule. In this section, we will investigate the significance of injury counteraction, dive into normal strength training wounds, and furnish you with the information and systems to limit risk and explore wounds.

Injury counteraction isn't only about staying away from disasters; it's tied in with cultivating a careful and adjusted way to deal with your wellness process. By figuring out how to safeguard your body and oversee wounds when they happen, you can guarantee that strength training stays a long-lasting, charming, and sans-injury try.

Common injuries in strength training

Strength training is an exceptionally compelling method for building muscle, further developing perseverance, and improving general fitness. Notwithstanding, similar to any active work, it conveys a risk of injury. Understanding the normal wounds that can happen during strength training, their causes, side effects, and counteraction methodologies is fundamental for guaranteeing a protected and helpful training experience. In this thorough aid, we'll investigate the most widely recognized wounds related to strength training and give experiences on the best way to forestall and oversee them.

1. Strains and Injuries

Causes: Strains happen when muscles or ligaments are extended past their cutoff points or torn. Hyperextends include tendons and come about because of the extending or tearing of these connective tissues. These wounds can occur because of inappropriate structure, lifting a lot of weight, or overexertion.

Side effects: Agony, expanding, and restricted scope of movement are ordinary side effects of strains and injuries. In extreme cases, there might be swelling or muscle fits.

Counteraction: Keep up with appropriate structure during workouts, warm up sufficiently, and try not to lift loads that are excessively weighty for your ongoing strength level. Steadily increase the power of your exercises and incorporate extending activities to develop adaptability further.

2. Tendonitis

Causes: Tendonitis is the irritation of a ligament, which interfaces muscle and bone. It can result from dull developments or abuse of a specific muscle bunch during strength training.

Side effects: Torment, delicacy, and enlarging around the impacted ligament are typical side effects of tendonitis. There may likewise be a greater scope of movement.

Counteraction: To forestall tendonitis, shift your activities to try not to abuse explicit muscles and ligaments. Focus on your body's signs and give it sufficient rest between exercises. Appropriate warm-ups and cool-downs are fundamental.

3. Rotator Sleeve Wounds

Causes: The rotator sleeve is a gathering of muscles and ligaments in the shoulder. Wounds to the rotator sleeve can happen because of ill-advised lifting methods, significant burdens, or abuse of the shoulder joint.

Side effects: Agony, shortcomings, and restricted scope of movement in the shoulder are demonstrative of rotator sleeve wounds. You may likewise encounter torment while lifting or coming.

Counteraction: Fortify the muscles around the shoulder joint, including the rotator sleeve, to offer better help. Utilize appropriate structure while performing shoulder exercises, and keep away from unreasonable or abrupt developments.

4. Back Wounds

Causes: Back wounds can result from poor lifting strategies, inappropriate structure, or utilizing a lot of weight during practices like deadlifts and squats. Circle hernia ion, a condition where the padding plates between the vertebrae get awkward, is an extreme back physical issue that can happen.

Side effects: Back wounds might cause agony, firmness, and muscle fits. On account of plate herniation, there may likewise be emanating torment, deadness, or shortcomings in the legs.

Counteraction

- Spotlight on keeping a nonpartisan spine position during practices that include the back.
- Utilize appropriate lifting strategies, and don't lift loads that are excessively weighty for your ability.
- Reinforce the center muscles to offer better support for your spine.

5. Knee Wounds

Causes: Knee wounds, for example, patellofemoral disorder or front cruciate tendon (leg tendon) tears, can happen because of ill-advised structure during practices like squats, jumps, or leg presses. Abuse and unreasonable weight on the knee joint can likewise prompt these wounds.

Side effects: Knee wounds might cause torment, expansion, shakiness, and trouble twisting or fixing the knee. On account of leg tendon tears, a popping sound or sensation at the hour of injury is normal.

Counteraction: Guarantee legitimate knee arrangement during workouts, and try not to overburden the knees with extreme weight. Reinforce the muscles around the knee joint, including the quadriceps and hamstrings, to give strength and backing.

6. Elbow Tendonitis (Tennis and Golf player's elbow)

Causes: Elbow tendonitis, otherwise called tennis elbow (parallel epicondylitis) or golf player's elbow (average epicondylitis), and happens because of abuse of the lower arm muscles and ligaments. It can result from monotonous holding, lifting, or contorting movements.

Side effects: Torment and delicacy on the external or inward side of the elbow are typical side effects of a tennis or golf player's elbow. These wounds may likewise cause shortcomings in the grasp.

Anticipation: Stay away from tedious holding developments and utilize appropriate structure during practices that include the lower arm muscles. Step by step, increase the power of your exercises and integrate lower arm strengthening activities.

7. Shin Braces

Causes: Shin braces, or average tibial pressure conditions, result from abuse or monotonous effects on the shinbone and the tissues that connect muscles deep down. This can occur in practices that include running or bouncing.

Side effects: Shin supports cause torment along the inward edge of the shinbone. The aggravation might be gentle at first, yet it can become severe in the event that it is not tended to.

Avoidance: Consolidate appropriate footwear with padding and curve support. Progressively increase the power and duration of high-influence activities to permit your body to adjust.

8. Wrist Wounds

Causes: Wrist wounds can happen during practices that include holding loads or coming down on the wrists, for example, seat presses or push-ups. Overextension of the wrist or utilizing an ill-advised structure can prompt injury.

Side effects: Torment, enlarging, and restricted scope of movement in the wrist are typical side effects of wrist wounds. You may likewise need help with your grasp.

Avoidance: Utilize legitimate structure and wrist support during practices that put the squeeze on the wrists. Reinforce the lower arm muscles to improve wrist dependability.

9. Parchedness and intensity-related wounds

Causes: Parchedness and intensity-related wounds can result from deficient liquid admission during exercises, particularly in hot and damp conditions. These wounds can range from a gentle lack of hydration to severe circumstances like intensity depletion or heatstroke.

Side effects: Drying out can cause side effects like unsteadiness, shortcoming, and squeezing. Heat depletion might prompt queasiness, weighty perspiring, and a quick heartbeat. Heatstroke is a health-related crisis and presents with side effects like disarray, high internal heat level, and loss of cognizance.

Avoidance: Remain all-around hydrated previously, during, and after your exercises, particularly in hot circumstances. Wear proper apparel and enjoy reprieves to chill off if essential.

10. Overtraining Disorder

Causes: Overtraining disorder results from extreme activity without sufficient rest and recovery. It can prompt physical and mental side effects, including exhaustion, muscle irritation, and state-of-mind unsettling influences.

Side effects: Overtraining can cause a range of side effects, including determined exhaustion, diminished execution, expanded defenselessness to disease, and changes in mindset, like crabbiness or wretchedness.

Counteraction

- Focus on rest and recovery in your training schedule.
- Guarantee you get sufficient rest and pay attention to your body's signs.
- Keep away from excessive training volume and power.

While strength training offers plenty of actual advantages, it's fundamental to approach it with care and watchfulness to forestall wounds. Understanding the average damages related to strength training, their causes, side effects, and counteraction systems is urgent for a protected and viable training venture. Recall that legitimate structure, slow movement, and satisfactory rest and recovery are critical variables in injury counteraction. If a physical problem arises, seek the appropriate medical attention and adhere to a well-planned recuperation schedule to safely resume training.

Warm-ups, cool-downs, and flexibility's role in injury prevention

In the domain of strength training, it is fundamental to defend your body against injuries. It's not just about the weight you lift or the redundancies you complete; it's likewise about how you plan and recuperate. Warm-ups, cool-downs, and adaptability prepare the structure as the center of injury anticipation, assuming parts that stretch beyond simple customs.

The Embodiment of Warm-Ups

Before you plunge into your strength instructional course, think about the warm-up as your body's delicate reminder. It facilitates your muscles and joints right into it. Through light, vigorous movements like lively strolling or cycling, your pulse steadily raises, your bloodstream increases, and your internal heat level hoists.

This steady shift from resting to dynamic mode is much the same as a symphony tuning its instruments before a presentation. Similarly, your warm-up prepares your muscles for the orchestra of developments they're going to embrace. Dynamic stretches, for example, leg swings or arm circles, further stir your body, upgrading muscle versatility.

The warm-up isn't simply physical; it's likewise a psychological change. As your pulse climbs and your muscles initiate, your center moves from the rest of the world to its primary job. This psychological readiness makes way for viable and safe activity.

The Imperative Job of Adaptability

Adaptability is your body's visa to a lengthy scope of movement, a quality critical for injury counteraction. With further developed adaptability, your joints can investigate their maximum capacity, and your muscles become more robust.

Through static stretching, you assist your body in arriving at new degrees of adaptability. Each stretch resembles a discourse between your muscles and your psyche, continuously growing your scope of movement. You target significant muscle gatherings, tending to areas of snugness that could, in some way or another, be injury areas of interest.

Adaptability isn't just about touch-your-toe gymnastics; it's about balance. Adjusted muscle adaptability forestalls uneven characters that could prompt unfortunate stances, inconvenience, or even injury. At the point when your muscles are one, they cooperate flawlessly, diminishing the risk of unnecessary weight on unambiguous regions.

The Worth of Cool-Downs

The end of your strength training meeting isn't the end goal; it's progress. Cool-downs are your delicate arrival after the elating exercise flight. Their motivation is to direct your body from effort back to a condition of rest.

As you finish up your meeting, your pulse stays raised. A cool-down assists it with step-by-step getting back to its resting rate. Sudden changes in pulse can prompt discombobulating or, in any event, blacking out, so this continuous plunge is fundamental.

In addition, your muscles, which have been buckling down, merit a snapshot of relief. A cool-down fills in as a cradle against post-exercise irritation. It works with the evacuation of byproducts like lactic corrosive while empowering supplement-rich blood to stream into your muscles.

Static stretches during your cool-down take the spotlight, focusing on the muscles you've drawn in during your exercise. They help in muscle recovery, loosening up your diligent muscle strands.

A Consistent Joining

Coordinating these components into your strength training routine isn't tied in with ticking checkboxes; it's tied in with making an agreeable stream. Your warm-up sets the stage, dynamically expanding in force to match the requests of your exercise. Dynamic stretches inside your introduction set up your muscles for activity.

Adaptability training need not be a different undertaking; it very well may be entwined with your day-to-day practice, your warm-up, or even your cool-down. By focusing on close or weak regions, you're cultivating flexibility.

The cool-down, frequently seen as an idea in retrospect, is your entryway to a protected plunge from the pinnacle of your exercise. It brings your pulse back to balance while offering your muscles a delicate goodbye.

Paying attention to your body is essential in the interim. It's a discussion where your body gives input, directing you on the span and force of your warm-up, the profundity of your stretches, and the beat of your cool-down.

For customized direction, particularly on the off chance that you're new to strength training, consider counseling a confirmed wellness coach or an actual specialist. They can make a warm-up, cool-down, and adaptability routine that line up with your objectives and unique requirements.

Consider warm-ups, cool-downs, and adaptability not as simple customs but rather as vital parts of your wellness process. They are the watchmen of your body, guaranteeing that your solidarity training stays protected, powerful, and sans injury. Consistency and tolerance are your partners in this way, where every component has its impact in fitting your body's orchestra of strength.

How to train around injuries

In the domain of strength training, wounds can put barriers down. Yet, with the right attitude and approach, they don't need to crash your fitness process altogether. Preparing around wounds isn't just imaginable; it can likewise be a chance for development and flexibility. In this aid, we'll investigate procedures and standards for training securely and effectively while managing wounds.

1. Look for Proficient Direction

Prior to diving into training for a physical issue, it's urgent to talk with a medical care professional or an actual specialist. They can give an exact finding, suggest the best game plan, and provide direction on what kinds of activities to stay away from or focus on. Your well-being and recuperation ought to constantly be the primary concern.

2. Grasp Your Physical issue

Information is power, particularly with regard to overseeing wounds. Carve out the opportunity to grasp the idea of your physical issue, its causes, and its restrictions. This understanding will illuminate your training changes and assist you with pursuing informed choices.

3. Train the Healthy Regions

While one piece of your body might be harmed, it doesn't mean you can't keep on dealing with different regions. Center around practices that don't irritate your physical issues. For example, on the off chance that you have a lower-body injury, consider chest-area exercises like seat presses, lines, or pull-ups.

4. Change Activities

As a rule, it's feasible to change activities to decrease the stress on the harmed region. For example, in the event that you have a wrist injury, you can switch from conventional push-ups to knee push-ups to lighten tension on your wrists. An actual specialist or coach can help with tracking down reasonable changes.

5. Lessen Power and Burden

Injury recuperation isn't an ideal opportunity to set individual records or push your lines. Decrease the force and heap of your activities to a level that permits you to perform them without torment or over-the-top strain. This could mean utilizing lighter loads or opposition groups, performing fewer redundancies, or diminishing the scope of movement.

6. Pay attention to Your Body

Torment is your body's approach to flagging that something is off-base. It's fundamental to separate between distress related to testing exercises and the aggravation brought about by your physical issue. On the off chance that an activity intensifies your physical problem or causes sharp torment, stop right away and look for direction on an elective methodology.

7. Focus on Recovery Activities

Consolidate recovery practices recommended by your medical services proficient or actual advisor into your daily schedule. These activities are explicitly intended to work with your recovery and reinforce the harmed region.

8. Steady Movement

As your physical issue progresses slowly, Try not to rush the cycle; your body needs time to adjust and recover strength. Steadily increment the power, length, and intricacy of your activities, yet consistently within the cutoff points set by your medical services proficiency.

9. Focus on Sustenance and Hydration

A reasonable eating regimen rich in supplements is fundamental for the mending system. Satisfactory protein consumption upholds tissue fix, while various nutrients and minerals assume vital parts in general well-being and healing. Remaining very hydrated is additionally imperative for ideal mending.

10. Rest and Recuperation

Give your body the rest it needs to recuperate. Quality rest and appropriate rest between exercises are fundamental for the mending system. Overtraining can block healing and increase the risk of additional injuries.

11. Keep a Positive Mentality

Wounds can be intellectually challenging. It's easy to become baffled or deterred; however, keeping a positive outlook is fundamental for progress. Center around what you can do instead of what you can't, and celebrate little triumphs en route.

12. Speak with Your Medical Services Group

Consistently update your medical care group, including your medical care supplier and actual specialist, on your advancement and any progressions in your condition. They can give direction, make adjustments to your treatment plan, and guarantee you're in good shape.

13. Think about Elective Modalities

Investigate elective treatments, for example, needle therapy, chiropractic care, or back rub medicine, in discussion with your medical services supplier. These modalities might assist with reducing torment and aid in the mending system.

14. Remain Predictable

Consistency is critical to injury recovery and, generally speaking, advancement. Adhere to your rescue and alter your workout routine tenaciously. The more predictable you are, the quicker and more viable your recovery is probably going to be.

15. Tolerance and long-haul point of view

Wounds can be misfortunes. However, they don't characterize your fitness process. Move toward your recuperation with persistence and a drawn-out point of view. Center around building severe strength areas for future advancement, regardless of whether it implies making a stride back briefly.

16. Try not to Rush the Return

At the point when you're prepared to get back to your ordinary training schedule, do so steadily and with alertness. Begin with lower loads and power and continuously work your direction back up. Hurrying the return can prompt re-injury.

Wounds can be tested, yet they don't need to mean certain death for your strength training venture. With a very educated and versatile methodology, you can keep on gaining ground, even while working around a physical issue. Continuously focus on your well-being and security, look for proficient direction, and keep a positive outlook. Recall that recuperation requires some investment, and the cycle might be slower than you'd like, yet with commitment and determination, you can defeat wounds and proceed with your way to strength and fitness.

CHAPTER 13

INCORPORATING CARDIO AND FLEXIBILITY

In the realm of strength training, it's easy to turn out to be exclusively centered on developing muscle and grit. I believe accomplishing a balanced and adjusted wellness routine includes something other than lifting loads. Cardiovascular activity and adaptability training are two fundamental parts that supplement your strength training endeavors, adding to general well-being, versatility, and life span.

In this section, we'll investigate the essential jobs that cardiovascular activity and strength training play in your fitness process. From upgrading your heart, well-being, and perseverance through cardio to working on your scope of movement and forestalling wounds with adaptability, you'll find how these components can raise your strength training experience. Whether you're a carefully prepared competitor or simply starting your wellness process, incorporating cardio and adaptability into your routine is a stage toward all-encompassing prosperity and fitness.

The role of cardiovascular training in a strength-focused routine

In the realm of fitness, the line between strength training and cardiovascular activity is unmistakable. Strength training typically includes lifting loads or performing obstruction activities to assemble muscle and power. Then again, cardiovascular conditioning, frequently known as cardio, underscores exercises that hoist your pulse and lift perseverance, like running, swimming, or cycling.

From the outset, these two wellness spaces conflict with one another. Strength training frequently consists of short eruptions of focused energy exertion, while cardio involves sustained, lower-power exercises that focus on perseverance. Notwithstanding, the collaboration between these apparently differentiating types of activity can be extraordinarily beneficial, prompting an all-encompassing wellness schedule.

Cardiovascular training, at its center, focuses on the well-being of your heart and circulatory framework. Taking part in cardio exercises builds your pulse and breathing rate, prompting a few key advantages:

1. Improved Heart Well-being: Cardio reinforces your heart, making it more proficient at siphoning blood and oxygen to your muscles and organs. It's a considerable partner in lessening the gamble of heart illnesses by further developing cholesterol levels and bringing down pulse.

2. **Enhanced Perseverance:** Customary cardio practices improve your endurance. This expanded perseverance permits you to participate in proactive tasks for stretched-out periods without surrendering to weakness. The perseverance help from cardiovascular training can definitely affect your presentation in strength instructional meetings.

3. **Calorie Consume:** Cardiovascular activities are famous for their calorie-consuming ability. When joined with a decent eating regimen, regular cardio can aid weight the board and fat misfortune, making it an essential part of an exhaustive wellness schedule.

Adjusting cardio and strength training isn't just imaginable but also exceptionally valuable. While strength training centers on building muscle and power, cardiovascular exercise tends to generally wellness and heart well-being. These two perspectives can complete one another, making an agreeable and hearty wellness schedule.

Cardiovascular training can upgrade your general wellness, permitting your body to proficiently ship oxygen and supplements to working muscles during strength instructional meetings. This enhancement prompts better execution and recovery in strength exercises.

Consolidating cardio into your wellness routine can help with post-strength training recuperation. Participating in light cardiovascular activities assists in eliminating metabolic byproducts by preferring lactic corrosive, decreasing post-exercise muscle irritation, and advancing quicker healing.

Also, cardiovascular training oversees weakness. At the point when your cardiovascular framework is robust, you can recuperate all the more rapidly between sets in strength training, keep up with appropriate structure, and lessen the gamble of injury.

Balance is vital when coordinating cardiovascular training into a strength-centered everyday practice. Here are a few down-to-earth tips:

1. Characterize Your Objectives: Your wellness goals ought to determine the harmony between cardio and strength training in your daily schedule. Assuming muscle building is your essential objective, center around strength training with moderate cardio for, generally speaking, wellness. For those planning to improve perseverance or get thinner, cardio may include a more significant piece of your daily schedule.

2. Shrewd Booking: Plan your exercises in a calculated way. You can dispense explicit days for strength training and others for cardiovascular training. Then again, integrate short cardio meetings as warm-ups or cool-downs for your solidarity exercises.

3. Assortment Matters: Keep your fitness routine drawing in and forestall levels by trying different things with various kinds of cardio. Whether it's stop-and-go aerobic exercise (HIIT) or consistent state running, assortment adds energy and keeps your body from adjusting excessively fast.

4. Stand by listening to Your Body: Focus on how your body answers different sorts and volumes of training. On the off chance that you sense indications of overtraining, like steady weakness, lessened execution, or state of mind aggravations, make essential acclimations to your daily practice. Rest and recovery are vital to your fitness process.

5. Focus on Nourishment and Hydration: Legitimate sustenance and hydration are imperative to help both cardiovascular and strength training. Guarantee your eating routine supplies the vital energy and supplements to fuel your exercises and advance recovery.

By maintaining an agreeable harmony between cardio and strength training, you can make a wellness schedule that advances muscle development and strength as well as upgrades generally perseverance, heart well-being, and prosperity. Collaboration offers the best-case scenario, lifting your fitness process higher than ever.

Static vs. dynamic stretching: When and how to use them

Extending is a fundamental piece of any fitness schedule, filling in as a way to upgrade adaptability, forestall wounds, and work on by and large, execution. Nonetheless, not all stretches are made equivalent, and figuring out the differentiation between static and dynamic extending, as well as knowing when and how to utilize each, can affect your exercise insight. In this chapter, we'll dive into the universe of extending, investigating the advantages and suitable uses of static and dynamic extending.

Static Extending the Exemplary Flex and Hold

Static extending is what the vast majority know all about. It includes lengthening a muscle to its farthest point and holding the stretch for a while, commonly 15 to 60 seconds. This technique plans to build the muscle's length and adaptability steadily. This is the way to integrate static extending into your routine, actually:

1. Warm up First: Static extending is best when your muscles are warm. Take part in light oxygen-consuming actions like running or hopping jacks for 5–10 minutes prior to beginning your static stretches. This increases the bloodstream to your muscles and makes them more flexible.

2. Hold, Don't Skip: While playing out a static stretch, arrive at a place of strain and stand firm on the footing without bobbing or jolting. Bobbing can prompt muscle strains or wounds.

3. Inhale and Unwind: While in the extended position, center around profound and controlled relaxation. This loosens up the muscles and empowers a more powerful stretch.

4. Target Explicit Muscles: Recognize the muscles you need to extend and choose proper static stretches. For instance, in the event that you're focusing on your quadriceps, a standing quad stretch is an exemplary static stretch.

5. Hold for Sufficient Time: To further develop adaptability, hold every static stretch for somewhere around 15–30 seconds, and bit by bit, moving gradually for as long as 60 seconds for more profound spaces. You can rehash it two to multiple times.

6. Incorporate full-body stretches: A balanced routine ought to incorporate static spaces for all significant muscle gatherings, including the hamstrings, calves, chest, shoulders, and back.

Advantages of Static Extending

Further developed Adaptability: Customary static extending can upgrade your general adaptability, making it simpler to perform ordinary errands and exercises with a more prominent scope of movement.

Injury Anticipation: Static extending lessens the gamble of wounds by stretching muscles and working on their flexibility. This is especially significant for exercises that include abrupt developments or high effects.

Upgraded Muscle Recuperation: Extending after an exercise can help with muscle recovery by diminishing muscle irritation and advancing unwinding.

Dynamic Extending: Adding Development to Your Warm-Up

Dynamic extending includes controlled developments that copy the activities you'll perform during your exercise. Dissimilar to static extending, dynamic stretches are active and have a progression of dull movements. This is the way to capitalize on unique extending:

1. Integrate into Warm-Up: Unique extending is excellent for heating up before an exercise. It readies your muscles for the particular developments and power of your instructional meeting.

2. Draw in the Entire Body: Dynamic extending schedules regularly include numerous muscle gatherings and joints. This heats individual muscles as well as supports coordination and equilibrium.

3. Step-by-step Increment Scope of Movement: Begin with little, controlled developments and continuously increment the scope of movement as your muscles warm up. This limits the gamble of overextending or stressing cold muscles.

4. Keep up with Controlled Speed: Dynamic extending ought to be performed with controlled, purposeful developments. Keep away from quick or jerky movements to forestall injury.

5. Designer to Your Movement: Pick dynamic stretches that line up with the exercises you'll perform. For instance, leg swings are appropriate for sports that include running and kicking, while arm circles are gainful for chest area commitment.

6. Rehash Developments: Dynamic stretches ought to be rehashed for around 8-12 redundancies for every set. You can play out numerous locations, continuously expanding the scope of movement with each group.

Advantages of Dynamic Extending

- **Improved Blood Stream:** Dynamic extending increments bloodstream to the muscles, assisting them with warm increasing rapidly and plan for work out.
- **Further developed Versatility**: These stretches center around utilitarian developments, improving joint portability and scope of movement.

- **Sport-Explicit Warm-Up:** Dynamic stretches can be custom-fitted to mirror the developments of your picked game or movement, giving a game explicit warm-up.
- **Injury Counteraction:** Like static extending, dynamic extending can assist with decreasing the gamble of injury by setting up your muscles for the requests of your exercise.

When to Utilize Each Extending Technique

Static Extending: Save static extending for your post-exercise routine everyday practice or during committed extending meetings. It's exceptionally viable for further developing adaptability and ought to be performed when your muscles are warm.

Dynamic Extending: Utilize dynamic extending as a feature of your warm-up everyday practice prior to taking part in more demanding activity. Dynamic stretches set up your muscles and joints for action, and going with them is an excellent decision for pre-exercise planning.

Consolidating Both into Your Everyday Practice

To receive the total rewards of extending:

- Consider integrating both static and dynamic extending into your fitness schedule.

- Begin with dynamic extending as a component of your warm-up, progressively changing into your exercise.
- Save static extending for your cool-down or as a different adaptability-centered meeting.

By understanding the distinctions between static and dynamic extending and knowing when and how to utilize every technique, you can streamline your extending routine to help your fitness objectives, further develop adaptability, forestall wounds, and improve general execution.

CHAPTER 14

TRACKING PROGRESS AND ADJUSTING YOUR PLAN

In the domain of strength training and fitness, progress isn't just about lifting heavier loads or running quicker miles; it's a powerful excursion of personal development, flexibility, and versatility. To explore this excursion successfully, you want a guide, and that is where the following advancement and changing your arrangement become integral factors.

This section investigates the vital job of checking your fitness process, setting attainable achievements, and making informed adjustments to your exercise and sustenance plans. Whether you're a fledgling hoping to fabricate strong groundwork or an accomplished competitor taking a stab at maximized execution, understanding how to follow progress and adjust your methodology is fundamental for proceeding with development and outcome in the realm of strength training and fitness.

The importance of logging workouts

Chasing fitness and strength training, consistency, and progress are critical. Accomplishing your fitness objectives requires devotion, exertion, and an essential methodology. One of the best devices for guaranteeing consistency and following advancement is logging your exercises. Whether you're a carefully prepared competitor or simply beginning your fitness process, keeping an exercise log can be a distinct advantage.

In this complete guide, we will dive into the significance of logging exercises. We'll investigate how keeping a nitty-gritty record of your instructional meetings can assist you with upgrading your fitness level, putting forth and accomplishing significant objectives, keeping away from classes, and, at last, receiving the benefits of your persistent effort.

1. Responsibility and Consistency

Consistency is the underpinning of any fruitful workout schedule. The paste holds your wellness process together. Logging your exercises gives you a sense of responsibility. At the point when you record every meeting, you're more averse to skipping exercises or cutting them off. Realizing that you're keeping track can give that additional inspiration to appear and do your absolute best reliably.

Consider your exercise log as a promise to yourself. It's an unmistakable indication of your fitness objectives, and every section is a stage toward accomplishing them. Over the long haul, this consistency compounds, prompting huge advancements in strength, perseverance, and overall fitness.

2. Objective Setting and Progress Following

One of the primary roles of logging exercises is to lie out and follow your wellness objectives successfully. Objectives provide your fitness process with motivation and a course. At the point when you have clear targets, your exercises become more engaging and intentional. This is the way an exercise log assists with objective setting and following advancement:

A. Laying out Brilliant Objectives: Shrewd represents explicit, quantifiable, attainable, applicable, and time-bound. Logging your exercises permits you to characterize objectives that meet these rules. For instance, rather than an unclear objective like "get more grounded," you can define a shrewd goal like "increment seat press max by 10 pounds in 12 weeks."

B. Following Advancement: Your exercise log fills in as a verifiable record of your wellness process. By consistently checking your catalog, you can perceive how far you've come. This gives a feeling of achievement as well as assists you with distinguishing regions where you might have to change your training or sustenance plan.

C. Changing Objectives: As you keep tabs on your development, you can find that a few objectives need change. You may be outperforming your underlying goals surprisingly quickly, or you've experienced unforeseen difficulties. Your exercise log empowers you to adjust your plans to mirror your developing wellness venture.

3. Objective Information and Customized training

Exercise logs give important objective information about your presentation. Rather than depending entirely on memory or discernment, you have substantial numbers and subtleties to reference. This information can illuminate your choices with respect to training power, practice determination, and recuperation methodologies:

A. Load Movement: By logging the weight lifted, redundancies, and sets for each activity, you can follow your movement after some time. This information assists you with deciding when now is the right time to expand the weight or force, guaranteeing you keep on testing your muscles and making gains.

B. Practice Choice: Your exercise log can uncover which activities yield the best outcomes for you. It permits you to recognize practices that might require adjustment or substitution. For instance, in the event that you reliably battle with a specific development, you can work with a mentor to see a reasonable other option.

C. Recuperation and Overtraining: Checking your training volume and power in your exercise log can assist you with keeping away from overtraining. Overtraining can prompt exhaustion, diminished execution, and even wounds. Perceiving examples of overtraining in your record permits you to change your training plan and focus on rest and recovery when required.

4. Inspiration and Representation

In some cases, remaining roused can be testing, particularly when progress appears to be slow or tricky. Your exercise log can act as a solid persuasive device in more than one way:

A. Noticeable Advancement: Glancing back at your past sections and contrasting them with your ongoing presentation can inconceivably rouse. It's unmistakable proof of your commitment and difficult work paying off.

B. Objective Representation: Your log can assist you with imagining your objectives. The point when you perceive that you are so near to accomplishing a specific achievement can support your assurance to push somewhat more enthusiastically and arrive at it.

C. Observing Accomplishments: As you accomplish your wellness objectives, your exercise log gives a record of those achievements. Praising your victories, regardless of how little, can build up your obligation to your wellness process.

5. Injury Avoidance and The executives

Keeping an exercise log can likewise play a part in physical issue counteraction, and the executives:

A. Following Torment or Distress: Assuming you experience agony or uneasiness during or after exercises, your log can help pinpoint when and where it happened. This data is significant while looking for guidance from a medical services professional or coach.

B. Recognizing Examples: An exercise log might uncover examples of abuse or burden on unambiguous muscles or joints. By perceiving these examples, you can make vital changes in accordance with your training routine to forestall wounds.

6. Nourishment and Recuperation Experiences

Your exercise log can remember notes for nourishment, rest, and recuperation systems. This all-encompassing methodology gives experiences into what these variables mean for your exhibition:

A. Sustenance: Recording your eating regimen when exercising can assist you with recognizing which food varieties fuel your exercises best. It can likewise feature any wholesome lack that might be influencing your energy levels and recovery.

B. Rest and Recuperation: Monitoring your rest examples and recuperation procedures can uncover their effect on your training. On the off chance that you perform well following a decent night's rest or specific recuperation rehearsals, you can integrate them into your standard all the more purposefully.

7. Responsibility and Backing

Sharing your exercise log with a mentor or exercise accomplice can improve responsibility and backing. They can survey your log, give direction, and gain proposals in light of your headway and objectives. Having somebody to share your fitness process with can propel and assist you with remaining focused.

Progress in the world of fitness and strength training is undoubtedly not a straight line but rather an adventure filled with challenges, successes, and improvement. An exercise log is your devoted friend on this excursion. An instrument keeps you responsible, helps you put forth and accomplish significant objectives, and gives essential experiences into your exhibition and progress.

Whether you're endeavoring to assemble muscle, further develop perseverance, or improve overall fitness, the demonstration of logging your exercises enables you to settle on informed choices, advance your training, and remain persuaded. It changes your fitness routine from a progression of activities into a deliberate and remunerating excursion of personal development. Thus, snatch a scratch pad or a fitness application, begin logging, and watch as your fitness yearnings become a substantial reality.

How to measure progress

Progress in your fitness process resembles the North Star directing your endeavors toward your objectives. Whether you intend to develop grit, gain muscle, further develop perseverance, or accomplish some other fitness objective, estimating your headway is essential for remaining focused and coming to informed conclusions about your training and sustenance. In this aid, we'll investigate different strategies to quantify progress in the domains of strength gains, muscle development, and general fitness.

1. Strength Gains Lifting the Heaviness of Progress

Strength is a vital part of fitness, and following your strength gains is fundamental for accomplishing your objectives. Here are viable ways of estimating your advancement in strength training:

A. One-Rep Max (1RM): The one-redundancy most extreme is the most significant weight you can lift for a solitary reiteration of a particular activity. Testing your 1RM intermittently permits you to perceive how your solidarity is working over the long run. Guarantee you play out these tests securely in a perfect world with a spotter.

B. Redundancy Max (RM): Instead of testing your 1RM, you can decide your 3RM, 5RM, or 10RM, which is the most significant weight you can lift for 3, 5, or 10 reiterations individually. Keeping tabs on your development in various rep ranges gives a far-reaching perspective on your solidarity gains.

C. Weight Movement: Monitoring the weight you use for different activities is a direct method for estimating progress. On the off chance that you reliably lift heavier loads or perform more redundancies with a given weight, it's an obvious sign of further developed strength.

D. Time Under Pressure (TUT): as well as lifting heavier loads, you can screen the time your muscles spend under strain during each set. Steadily expanding TUT, either through more slow reiterations or additional challenging activities, can prompt strength gains.

E. Movement in Exercise Trouble: Progressing to additional complex varieties of activities is one more indication of progress. For instance, advancing from standard push-ups to precious stone push-ups or from bodyweight squats to gun squats exhibits expanded strength and control.

2. Muscle Development: Past the Mirror

Building muscle improves your physical makeup as well as adds to practical strength and, in general, well-being. This is the way you can quantify progress in muscle development:

A. Bigness Estimations: Estimating the outline of explicit body parts, like your biceps, thighs, or midsection, permit you to follow changes in muscle size. Utilize an adaptable measuring tape, and guarantee consistency in estimation focuses.

B. Progress Photographs: Routinely taking photographs from different points can give visual proof of muscle development. Contrasting pictures over the long run can uncover unpretentious changes that may not be promptly clear in the mirror.

C. Body Synthesis Examination: Procedures like skin fold caliper estimations or further developed techniques like DEXA outputs can survey changes in body pieces, including bulk and muscle versus fat ratio.

D. Weight Gain: While not the sole mark of muscle development, an expansion in body weight, particularly when joined by an organized strength training program and legitimate sustenance, can recommend muscle gain.

E. Strength Movement: As referenced previously, an expansion in strength frequently goes with muscle development. Assuming that you're lifting continuously heavier loads, almost certainly your muscles are also developing.

3. Perseverance and Cardiovascular fitness

Perseverance and cardiovascular wellness are fundamental for exercises that require sustained exertion. Estimating progress in this space is similarly significant.

A. Time and Distance: In the event that you're a sprinter, cyclist, or swimmer, following the time it takes to finish a particular distance or the distance canvassed in a set time period is a straightforward method for estimating perseverance progress.

B. Pulse Recuperation: Checking your pulse healing can give you experiences in your cardiovascular wellness. A speedier revisitation of your resting pulse after practice demonstrates further developed perseverance.

C. Vo2 Max: Vo2 max is a proportion of your body's most excellent oxygen utilization during exercise. As it builds, your vigorous limit and perseverance get to the next level. Particular fitness appraisals or wearable gadgets can assess your Vo2 max.

D. Pace of Seen Effort (RPE): Abstract input matters. Focus on how exercises feel. As you progress, you should see that a similar degree of power feels less testing over the long haul.

4. Adaptability and Portability: The Opportunity to Move

Adaptability and portability are, in many cases, disregarded yet fundamental parts of, generally speaking, wellness. Estimating progress here forestalls wounds and further develops development quality:

A. Scope of Movement (ROM) Tests: Direct unambiguous scope of movement tests for different joints and developments.

Consistently retesting and taking note of upgrades can show expanded adaptability and versatility.

B. Practical Development Screens: Utilitarian development evaluations, similar to the Useful Development Screen (FMS), can recognize development lacks and awkward natures. By retesting and resolving these issues, you can further develop portability and diminish the risk of injury.

C. Yoga and Extending Movement: On the off chance that you practice yoga or commit time to extending schedules, you can quantify progress by following your capacity to perform further developed poses or accomplish further stretches after some time.

D. Decreased Distress: Further developed adaptability and portability frequently lead to diminished inconvenience or agony during everyday exercises. Following decreases in distress can be an indication of progress.

5. In General Wellness and Prosperity

Estimating progress in strength, muscle development, perseverance, and adaptability is fundamental; however, remember the master plan—your general wellness and prosperity:

A. Rest Quality: Quality rest is essential for healing and, generally speaking, well-being. Following your rest designs and taking note of enhancements in rest quality can, in a roundabout way, demonstrate better wellness.

B. Energy Levels: As your fitness improves, you ought to encounter higher energy levels throughout the day. Further developed energy can be a significant mark of general wellness progress.

C. State of mind and mental prosperity: customary activity significantly affects psychological wellness. Following your temperament and mental prosperity can assist you in perceiving the positive effects of your wellness schedule.

D. Well-being Markers: Watch out for fundamental well-being markers like pulse, cholesterol levels, and glucose. There can be areas of strength for, generally speaking, and fitness progress.

Estimating progress in your fitness process isn't restricted to a solitary measurement. It's a diverse methodology that considers different parts of your physical and mental prosperity. By keeping tabs on your development in strength gains, muscle development, perseverance, adaptability, and general wellness, you gain an extensive comprehension of your excursion's direction.

Recall that progress may be more complex than 100% of the time. Levels and misfortunes are essential for the interaction, yet they can likewise act as significant opportunities for growth.

Consistency, persistence, and a comprehensive way to deal with estimating progress will keep you spurred and informed on your way to accomplishing your wellness objectives.

Adjusting your training based on feedback and results

Adjusting your training in light of criticism and results is an essential part of accomplishing your fitness objectives. Whether you fabricate muscle, increment strength, further develop perseverance, or improve general fitness, a viable training program should advance over the long haul to keep you tested and advancing. In this aid, we'll investigate the specialty of changing your training in light of criticism and results, guaranteeing that your fitness process stays dynamic and successful.

1. Customary Appraisal

To make informed adjustments to your training, you first need solid criticism. Customary evaluations are the foundation of this cycle. This is the way to make a compelling criticism circle:

A. Survey Your Objectives: Start by returning to your fitness objectives. Is it true that they are as yet lined up with your goals and needs? Your dreams might develop over the long haul, so it's essential to guarantee they mirror your ongoing goals.

B. Track Progress: As examined in a past aide, it is imperative to keep tabs on your development. Screen key pointers, for example, strength gains, muscle development, perseverance enhancements, and other significant measurements in view of your objectives. Consistently record this information in an exercise log or wellness application.

C. Stand by listening to your body. Focus on how your body answers the questions. Are you encountering determined weariness, muscle touchiness, or inconvenience? Your body's signs can provide essential bits of knowledge about your training's adequacy.

D. Look for Proficient Direction: Consider talking with a fitness expert or mentor to evaluate your structure, method, and, by and large, advancement. They can offer master bits of knowledge and changes customized to your particular requirements.

2. Changing Training Factors

When you have criticism and results close by, now is the right time to change your training actors. These factors incorporate force, volume, recurrence, and exercise choice. This is the way to adjust them successfully:

A. Power: Force alludes to how testing an activity is. To increase power, you can lift heavier loads, increase opposition, or abbreviate rest periods between sets. Assuming your objective is strength or muscle gain, steadily expanding capacity is fundamental.

B. Volume: Volume is the aggregate sum of work you do in an exercise, commonly estimated in sets and reiterations. Changing volume includes adding or decreasing locations and redundancies. Expanding volume can animate muscle development while diminishing it could be fundamental for recovery.

C. Recurrence: Recurrence alludes to how frequently you train. Changing recurrence can assist you with overseeing responsibility and recovery. For example, you could add or eliminate training days in view of your objectives and recuperation limit.

D. Practice Choice: Intermittently change your activity determination to forestall levels and keep your exercises locking in. For instance, assuming you've been zeroing in on free-weight squats, you can switch to front squats or rushes to target muscles distinctively.

3. Periodization Organized Movement

Periodization is an organized way to deal with changing your training in light of explicit periods or stages. It assists you with burning through various training powers and objectives to forestall stagnation. There are different periodization models, including direct, undulating, and block periodization. Here is an improved outline:

A. Direct Periodization: This approach includes slowly expanding force and diminishing volume north of a little while or months. It's usually utilized for strength training, with each stage extending to the past one.

B. Undulating Periodization: Otherwise called everyday undulating periodization (DUP), this technique shifts back and forth between various training forces. For instance, you could have weighty, moderate, and light days. DUP is viable for keeping up with the assortment and preventing abuse wounds.

Block Periodization: In block periodization, training is separated into unmistakable blocks, each zeroing in on unambiguous angles like strength, hypertrophy, or power. This approach takes into consideration a profound spotlight on one objective prior to continuing to the following.

4. Recuperation and De loading

Changing your training isn't just about expanding force; it's likewise about knowing when to tone it down. Consolidating recuperation periods and deloading weeks is pivotal for long-haul progress:

A. Dynamic Recuperation: Integrate dynamic recuperation days or weeks into your training plan. These periods include lower-power exercises like swimming, yoga, light cycling, and advancing recuperation without complete rest.

B. Deloading: Deloading weeks include decreasing training volume and power to permit your body to recuperate completely. During deloading, you can diminish the weight lifted, perform fewer sets, or take more expanded rest periods.

5. Paying Attention to Your Body

While organized changes and periodization are significant, paying attention to your body stays vital. Your body gives criticism as touchiness, exhaustion, and energy levels. This is the way to answer:

A. Oversee Weariness: Persevering weakness can be an indication of overtraining. Assuming you're feeling reliably drained and execution is declining, integrating more rest and recovery into your routine is fundamental.

B. Address Inconvenience: Focus on distress or agony. Pain during exercise is normal, yet determined or intense torment might demonstrate an issue that requires rest or clinical consideration.

C. Adjust to Life Changes: Life-altering situations, like work responsibilities, travel, or ailment, can disturb your training schedule. In such cases, it's fundamental to change your training in like manner and try not to propel yourself when your body needs rest or recovery.

D. Rest When Required: Rest is a pivotal piece of progress. Pay attention to your body's prompts and permit yourself to rest when essential. Rest days are not difficulties but instead open doors for development and healing.

The Craft of Movement

Changing your training in view of criticism and results is both a science and a craft. It includes organized approaches like periodization, changing training factors, and integrating recuperation methodologies. In any case, it likewise depends on your instinct and capacity to pay attention to your body.

Recall that progress isn't generally direct, and misfortunes are a characteristic of any wellness venture. Embrace the cycle, remain versatile, and keep gaining from your encounters. With the proper harmony between design and adaptability, you can accomplish your wellness objectives and partake in a supportive, compensating excursion of personal development.

CHAPTER 15

CELEBRATING STRENGTH - STORIES FROM REAL WOMEN

Strength isn't just about actual power; it's an indication of flexibility, assurance, and the ability to overcome difficulties. In this chapter, we praise the strength of genuine women from assorted foundations and different backgrounds. Their accounts move us to get through boundaries, break generalizations, and rethink the significance of power.

As we dig into the stories of these extraordinary women, you'll observe the groundbreaking force of solidarity in the entirety of its structures. These accounts are a demonstration of the human soul's ability to endure and transcend difficulty, whether it's in the rec center, in the work environment, or even with life's most impressive preliminaries.

Plan to be animated, moved, and inspired as we commend the strength that lives inside each woman and the unimaginable excursions that lead them to where they are today. These accounts are a demonstration of the staggering potential inside every one of us to accomplish significance, regardless of the deterrents we experience en route.

Inspirational stories of women who transformed their lives through strength training

Strength training isn't just about lifting loads; it's an excursion of self-disclosure, strengthening, and change. For women, specifically, it can break generalizations, support certainty, and work on, by and large, prosperity. In this part, we'll investigate the moving accounts of women who exploit the advantages of strength training to change their lives.

1. Sarah's Excursion: From Weakness to Certainty

Sarah's story starts with a recognizable battle. She had consistently had an uncertain outlook on her body, frequently contrasting herself with ridiculous excellence guidelines. At some point, she concluded the time had come to roll out an improvement. Sarah set out on a strength-building excursion to develop actual grit as well as mental versatility.

As she advanced in her exercises, Sarah found the delight of testing herself and accomplishing achievements. The feeling of accomplishment she felt in the rec center transformed into expanded trust in different aspects of her life. She began putting forth aggressive professional objectives and sought after her interests with recently discovered assurance. Sarah's story is a demonstration of how strength training can enable women to break free from self-uncertainty and seek after their fantasies with faithful certainty.

2. Maya's Victory over Difficulty

Maya's strength training venture is one of versatility and win-over affliction. She confronted a progression of extraordinary mishaps, including a problematic illness and a troublesome separation. These difficulties left her inclination genuinely and sincerely drained. Not entirely set in stone to recover her life, Maya went to strength training.

Beginning with essential activities, she steadily developed her actual fortitude and endurance. In any case, more critically, strength training turned into her haven, where she could recapture her feeling of control and certainty. With each rep and set, Maya's soul developed further, and she rose out of her battles with newly discovered versatility. Her story fills in as an update that strength training isn't just about actual change but also about reconstructing one's life from the back to the front.

3. Maria's Strengthening Through Weightlifting

Maria's excursion into the universe of strength training started when she coincidentally found a weightlifting class at her neighborhood rec center. Fascinated, she chose to check it out. Much to her dismay, this choice would prompt a significant change.

Through weightlifting, Maria developed actual grit as well as mental mettle. She figured out how to embrace difficulties and stretch her boundaries, both in the exercise center and in her own life. Maria's story features the way that strength training can enable women to face challenges, embrace their inward champion, and face life's vulnerabilities with faithful fortitude.

4. Lisa's Story: Defeating Self-perception Issues

For Lisa, strength training was a lifesaver out of the ocean of self-perception that had tormented her for quite a long time. She had struggled with dietary issues and confidence challenges, which altogether affected her general prosperity.

At the point when Lisa began strength training, it was a disclosure. It permitted her to move her concentration from accomplishing a specific body shape to becoming more grounded and better. With the backing of a proficient coach, she found out about legitimate sustenance and the significance of taking care of oneself.

After some time, Lisa's body changed, but more critically, so did her relationship with herself. She started to see the value in her body for what it could do, as opposed to what it looked like. Lisa's story is a demonstration of the recuperating force of solidarity preparing and its capability to reshape bodies as well as brains.

5. Effortlessness' Excursion: Tracking down Autonomy

Elegance's story is tied to acquiring actual strength as well as the autonomy she had long wanted. As a single parent, she frequently felt overpowered by the demands of work and nurturing. She longed to be independent and solid.

Strength training turned into Effortlessness's way to autonomy. Through predictable exercises, she developed the actual fortitude expected to handle everyday assignments effortlessly. Moreover, the psychological versatility she acquired helped her face life's difficulties head-on.

Today, Effortlessness isn't just genuinely more grounded but additionally sincerely engaged. She is a brilliant illustration of how strength training can assist women with accomplishing a degree of independence that changes their lives.

Strength Past the Free weight

These accounts of change through strength training feature the extraordinary power it holds for women. It's not simply about chiseling muscles or accomplishing a specific style; it's about strengthening, self-disclosure, and the enduring conviction that women can beat any snag that life tosses their direction.

Strength training is a vehicle for change, an instrument that empowers women to fabricate physical and mental flexibility, overcome self-questioning, and arise as their best selves. These persuasive women advise us that, past the free weight, there lies a universe of vast conceivable outcomes and the solidarity to hold onto them. Their processes act as encouraging signs, directing women of any age and foundation toward a way of strengthening and changing.

How strength training empowers women in various aspects of life

Strength training isn't just about lifting loads; a groundbreaking excursion engages women in endless ways. Past-developing actual fortitude improves mental strength, helps certainty, and definitely influences different parts of life. In this investigation, we'll dig into how strength training enables women in other aspects of their lives.

1. Certainty and Confidence

As women vanquish new difficulties and accomplish actual achievements, they gain a profound sense of accomplishment. This freshly discovered certainty frequently reaches out to different everyday issues, like the working environment and individual connections.

Strength training instructs women that they are able to do more than they might have recently accepted. As they witness their bodies develop further, they become engaged to handle life's difficulties with more prominent self-assuredness. This change in outlook can prompt expanded confidence, better direction, and an eagerness to pursue new open doors.

2. Actual Well-being and Health

Strength training contributes to actual well-being and general health. It helps women fabricate and keep up with slender bulk, which can prompt a higher resting metabolic rate and further develop body structure. Furthermore, strength training:

- **Improves Bone Thickness:** As women age, keeping up severe strength areas becomes significant. Strength training animates bone development and forestalls conditions like osteoporosis.
- **Further develops Stance:** A solid center and adjusted muscle structure advance a better stance, diminishing the gamble of constant back and neck torment.
- **Upgrades Cardiovascular Well-being:** While not a substitution for cardiovascular activity, strength training can assist with bringing down pulse and further develop heart well-being.
- **Oversees Weight**: Muscle consumes a more significant number of calories than fat, making it simpler to oversee weight and body piece.
- **Diminishes the Gamble of Injury**: Reinforcing muscles and connective tissues can decrease the gamble of injury during ordinary exercises and sports.

3. Mental Flexibility and Stress The board

The psychological advantages of strength training are as critical as the actual ones. The discipline expected for steady gym routines develops mental flexibility and assurance. Women who participate in strength training frequently report:

- **Stress Decrease**: Active work, including strength training, triggers the arrival of endorphins, which can lighten pressure and further develop temperament.
- **Worked on Mental Durability:** Pushing through testing exercises encourages mental strength and the capacity to drive forward despite misfortune.
- **Upgraded Concentration and Fixation**: Strength training requires concentration and focus, which can extend to different parts of life, including work and scholastics.
- **Expanded Self-restraint**: The propensity for customary activity ingrains self-control, a significant quality for accomplishing both present moment and long haul objectives.

4. Strengthening in the Work environment

Strength training can significantly affect women' expert lives. The self-assurance and mental flexibility created through strength training can prompt professional development and achievement. Women who strength trains frequently report:

- **Upgraded Authority Abilities**: Expanded certainty and self-assuredness can make women more successful forerunners in the work environment.
- **Better Pressure the executives:** The capacity to oversee pressure through exercise can mean superior execution under tension.
- **Expanded Energy**: Strength preparing can support energy levels, assisting women with remaining on track and valuable all through the working day.
- **Viable Using time effectively:** The obligation to standard exercises cultivates successful time usage abilities, which can be crucial in adjusting work and individual life.

5. Building Solid, Encouraging groups of people

Strength training frequently happens in a steady local area, whether at an exercise center, in bunch classes, or through web-based fitness networks. These organizations offer support, fellowship, and a feeling of having a place. Women who strength trains frequently find:

- **Positive Social Associations:** Building associations with similar people who share fitness objectives can prompt enduring kinships and a feeling of the local area.
- **Mentorship and Motivation:** Inside these organizations, women frequently find guides and

wellsprings of motivation, which can significantly affect their own proficient lives.
- **Responsibility:** Preparing with a gathering or accomplice gives responsibility, making it more probable that women will adhere to their fitness schedules.

6. Body Inspiration and Self-Acknowledgment

Strength training advances a positive relationship with one's body. Women figure out how to see the value in their bodies for their abilities as opposed to their appearance. This change in context can prompt more noteworthy body energy and self-acknowledgment. Women frequently find:

- **An Emphasis on Usefulness:** Strength training underscores what the body can do, moving the concentration away from cultural magnificence norms.
- **Diminished Body Disgrace:** As women witness their bodies become more grounded, they frequently experience decreased sensations of disgrace or deficiency.
- **Expanded Body Certainty:** More noteworthy strength and fitness can help body certainty, prompting really satisfying individual connections and working on mental self-portraits.

Engaging Women, Each Rep In turn

Strength training engages women in many ways, from improving actual well-being and mental versatility to cultivating self-assurance and moving proficient development. Past the substantial advantages, it furnishes women with an all-encompassing way to deal with personal growth and a feeling of strengthening that penetrates all parts of life.

As women keep on embracing the force of solidarity preparing, they break generalizations, break obstructions, and reclassify significant areas of strength for being. Every rep, each set, and every exercise turns into a demonstration of their versatility and assurance, advising them that they are fit for accomplishing significance, both inside and outside the rec center.

CONCLUSION

In the excursion we've set out upon through the pages of this book, we've investigated the extraordinary force of solidarity preparing for women. A tour rises above the bounds of the rec center, venturing into each part of life and engaging women to turn into the engineers of their predeterminations.

Strength training, frequently seen as a way to shape a more muscular build, arises as a power that enables women genuinely, intellectually, and inwardly. A device encourages versatility, certainty, and the immovable conviction that women can vanquish any test, whether it's lifting loads or getting through cultural boundaries.

We've dug into a bunch of ways in which strength training improves actual well-being as well as mental prosperity. It constructs ground work of certainty, not established exclusively in appearances but instead in the comprehension of one's capacities. With each set and rep, women gain a recently discovered identity assuredness that stretches out into all features of life.

The tales of genuine women who've bridled the force of solidarity preparing act as reference points of motivation. These accounts advise us that strength isn't just about the weight lifted or the muscle constructed; it's about the grit to revise one's story, break liberated from self-uncertainty, and seek after dreams with enduring assurance.

Strength training is wider than age, foundation, or situation. A general language rises above limits, interfacing with women from varying backgrounds. Through the securities shaped in exercise centers, fitness classes, and online networks, women track down help as well as mentorship and motivation, driving them toward their objectives.

As we finish up this excursion, we're left with a significant comprehension: strength is definitely not a one-layered idea bound to genuineness. A power engages women to beat misfortune, accomplish self-disclosure, and flourish in each part of life.

May the insight partook in these pages keep on rousing, guiding, and elevating women as they embrace their solidarity, shape their predeterminations, and commend the wonderful excursion of self-disclosure and strengthening that is strength preparing. Keep in mind your process has just barely started, and with each rep, you're one bit nearer to turning into the most grounded adaptation of yourself all around. Embrace strength, and let it shape your life in manners you won't ever envision.

www.ingramcontent.com/pod-product-compliance
Lightning Source LLC
LaVergne TN
LVHW020929090426
835512LV00020B/3280